INSIDE

LANGUAGE · LITERACY · CONTENT

NATIONAL GEOGRAPHIC LEARNING | CENGAGE Learning

INSIDE

LANGUAGE · LITERACY · CONTENT

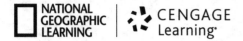

Acknowledgments

Grateful acknowledgment is given to the authors, artists, photographers, museums, publishers, and agents for permission to reprint copyrighted material. Every effort has been made to secure the appropriate permission. If any omissions have been made or if corrections are required, please contact the Publisher.

Photographic Credits

Cover, Back Cover ©Patrick Endres/Visuals Unlimited/ Corbis. **1** ©New Stock/Alamy. **13** ©Image Source Black/ Jupiterimages. **27** ©Rob Watkins/PYMCA/Jupiterimages. **29** (tl) ©DLILLC/Corbis. **29** (tr) ©Digital Vision/Alamy. **29** (bl) ©Archivberlin Fotoagentur GmbH/Alamy. **29** (br) ©Comstock Images/Jupiterimages. **32** ©Patrick Sheandell O' Carroll/PhotoAlto Agency/Jupiterimages. **104** ©Frank Whitney/The Image Bank/Getty Images. **112** ©Roger Ressmeyer/Corbis. **114** (c) ©Phil Schermeister/Corbis. **114** (bkgd) ©The Stocktrek Corp/Brand X/Jupiterimages. **167** ©DLILLC/Corbis.

For product information and technology asistance, contact us at
Cengage Learning Customer & Sales Support, 1-800-354-9706

For permission to use material from this text or product, submit all requests online at **www.cengage.com/permissions**
Further permissions questions can be emailed to
permissionrequest@cengage.com

National Geographic Learning | Cengage Learning
1 Lower Ragsdale Drive
Building 1, Suite 200
Monterey, CA 93940

Cengage Learning is a leading provider of customized learning solutions with office locations around the globe, including Singapore, the United Kingdom, Australia, Mexico, Brazil, and Japan. Locate your local office at **www.cengage.com/global**.

Visit National Geographic Learning online at **ngl.cengage.com**
Visit our corporate website at **www.cengage.com**

Printer: RR Donnelley, Harrisonburg, VA

ISBN: 978-12854-39020 (Writer's Workout)
ISBN: 978-12854-39051 (Writer's Workout Teacher's Annotated Edition)

ISBN: 978-12857-55076 (Writer's Workout Practice Masters)
Teachers are authorized to reproduce the practice masters in this book in limited quantity and solely for use in their own classrooms.

Printed in the United States of America
13 14 15 16 17 18 19 20 21 22
10 9 8 7 6 5 4 3 2 1

Contents

Table of Contents, continued

Editing and Proofreading Marks

Mark	Meaning	Example
∧	Insert something.	This lake is beautful. (insert *i*)
∧	Add a comma.	I love to fish but I can't do it often.
⌃	Add a semicolon.	I've never seen the Pacific Ocean I've heard it is amazing.
⊙	Add a period.	I love going to the beach
⊙	Add a colon.	The tide comes in at 7:30.
ⱽ ⱽ	Add quotation marks.	She yelled, What a view!
ⱽ	Add an apostrophe.	Anns pool is never clean.
≡	Capitalize.	It barely rains in the mojave desert.
/	Make lowercase.	I usually sit under Trees for shade.
ℛ	Delete, take something out.	My friend lives on an islands.
¶	Make new paragraph.	"I just saw a salmon!" I shouted. ¶ "Where?" he asked.
◯	Spell out.	My mom has been to the (U.S.)
⌃	Replace with this.	His best friend is a cat. (replace with *dog*)
∿	Change order of letters or words.	My aunt's garden is really nice, but it takes a (time long) to water.
#	Insert space.	Whales are mammals that live in the ocean. (insert #)
◡	Close up, no space here.	I went to the aquarium to day.

Sentences and Paragraphs

What makes this paragraph a good model?
Read the paragraph and answer the questions.

Dog Person
by Trish Smith

   I am very good with dogs. I just get along well with them, and they really seem to listen to me. I've trained my dog to sit, stay, and do tricks. I taught my neighbor's dog to walk without tugging. Now I'm helping my friend Anna train her dog, too.

Feature Checklist

A good paragraph

☐ has a topic sentence that states the main idea

☐ contains details that tell more about the main idea.

1. Does this paragraph have a topic sentence?

_____

_____

_____

2. What main idea is stated in the topic sentence?

_____

_____

_____

3. How do the paragraph's details tell more about the main idea?

_____

_____

_____

_____

_____

4. Should the writer add a sentence to explain that she likes horses, too? Why or why not?

_____

_____

_____

_____

_____

_____

State a Topic Sentence

Look at the following writing topics and details. Once you see how the details fit with the topic, write a good topic sentence for each example.

Paragraph 1

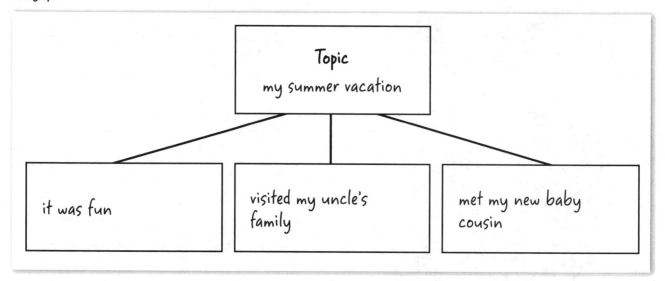

Topic Sentence:

_____

_____

Paragraph 2

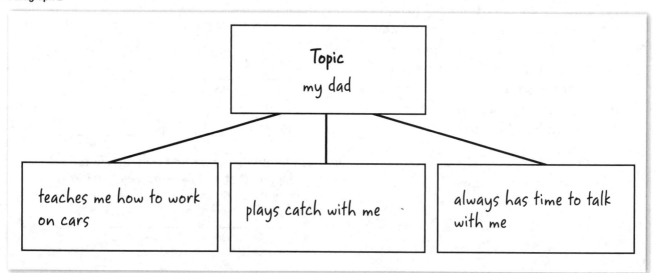

Topic Sentence:

_____

_____

Plan and Write a Paragraph

Use pages 3–4 to plan and write a paragraph that tells one important idea about who you are.

1. What do you most want your readers to know? List some ideas below. Decide what you want to emphasize. Then, circle the topic you've chosen.

   _____

   _____

   _____

   _____

2. Now that you have chosen a topic, list details that relate to it. Your details will show how you are this type of person.

   _____

   _____

   _____

   _____

3. To plan your paragraph, use this graphic organizer to get your thoughts in order. Write your main idea first. Then add details, or examples.

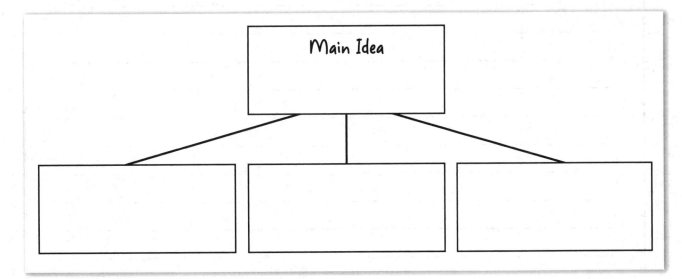

4. Write a topic sentence that connects your main idea and details.

   _____

   _____

5. Use your graphic organizer on page 3 to write a paragraph. Write your topic sentence. Then turn your details into sentences that help to prove your main idea.

Revise a Paragraph

1. Use the checklist to evaluate this draft of a paragraph. What changes are needed?

_____

_____

_____

_____

© National Geographic Learning, a part of Cengage Learning, Inc.

Revising Checklist

☐ Does your topic sentence state your main idea?

☐ Do you need to add any more examples?

☐ Are there any parts that are confusing or unclear?

☐ Are the sentences in the most effective order?

2. Revise the draft. Use revising marks to show your changes.

Revising

MARK	WHAT IT MEANS
∧	Insert something.
↶	Move to here.
∧—	Replace with this.
⏤ｅ	Take out.
¶	Make a new paragraph.

My American Football Experience

I did not understand American football when I first came to this country. Soccer and basketball are the two most popular sports. Last night I went to an American football game. It was the first time I experienced American football in person. I did not understand the rules. I went with a friend from school. He showed me where to buy food for the game. We ate snacks, like pretzels and popcorn.

3. Now use the checklist to help you revise the draft of your paragraph on page 4. Use a clean sheet of paper.

Edit and Proofread

Mechanics Workout: Check for Correct Sentences

Find and fix any errors in sentence capitalization or punctuation.

Editing and Proofreading Marks

∧	Insert something.
⋀	Add a comma.
⋀	Add a semicolon.
⊙	Add a period.
⊙	Add a colon.
⌄ ⌄	Add quotation marks.
⌄	Add an apostrophe.
≡	Capitalize.
╱	Make lower case.
℘	Delete.
¶	Make new paragraph.
◯	Check spelling.
⌒	Replace with this.
∿	Change order.
#	Insert space.
⌒	Close up.

First Friend

My best friend, Gina, really helped me adjust to a new life at a new school. my family moved all the way across the country to Virginia Beach? i didn't have any friends at my new school For the first few weeks, no one would sit at the lunch table with me. Can you believe that Then one day, Gina saw me sitting by myself. she introduced herself and asked if I was the new girl? We've been best friends ever since

Edit and Proofread Your Paragraph

Now edit and proofread your work.

1. Use a checklist as you edit and proofread. Add things you are working on to the checklist.

2. Look to see which errors are marked most often. Jot down your top three trouble spots.

Remember to Check

- ☐ capitalization
- ☐ periods for statements or commands
- ☐ punctuation marks for other sentence types
- ☐ _____
- ☐ _____

_____

_____

_____

3. Ask your teacher about ways to fix these errors, or see the Grammar Handbook.

Plan and Write a Persuasive Paragraph

Choose a place that you think is a great place to live. Plan and write a persuasive paragraph to tell why it is a great place to live.

1. Organize your ideas in a diagram. Write your claim in the top box of the diagram. List your reasons and evidence in the two columns.

Claim

Reasons	Evidence

Use your diagram on page 9 and follow these steps to write your paragraph on the lines below.

2. Write a sentence to introduce your claim. Name the place you will be telling about. State your idea about the place.

3. Add reasons to support your claim. Make sure your reasons are clear and specific.

4. Include evidence from credible sources to further support your claim.

Claim idea that you want to convince others to believe and support

Reasons tell readers why they should agree with your claim

Evidence gives facts or data to support your claim

Revise a Persuasive Paragraph

1. Evaluate this draft of a persuasive paragraph. What changes are needed?

_____

_____

_____

_____

_____

Feature Checklist

A good persuasive paragraph

☐ introduces a claim

☐ presents clear reasons and relevant evidence to support the claim

2. Revise the draft. Use revising marks to show your changes.

Revising

MARK	WHAT IT MEANS
∧	Insert something.
↶	Move to here.
⌐	Replace with this.
ϱ	Take out.
¶	Make a new paragraph.

Life in a Big City

A big city has a lot to offer. Many people move to a big city, like Chicago or Dallas, because there are more jobs there than in smaller towns. It is also easy for people to travel in a city because there are many ways. You can take a train, subway, bus, or cab to get where you need to go. And there are always places to go in a big city. For example, New York City has several public parks and many theaters where you can see a play or musical. Because so many people live in a city, it is very easy to meet. Most cities have plenty of clubs and groups where you can find people who like the same things you do. Living in a big city has many advantages.

3. Now use the checklist to help you revise the draft of your persuasive paragraph on page 10. Use a clean sheet of paper.

Edit and Proofread

Mechanics Workout: Check for Correct Sentences

Find and fix any errors in sentence capitalization and punctuation.

Editing and Proofreading Marks	
∧	Insert something.
⋏	Add a comma.
⋏	Add a semicolon.
⊙	Add a period.
⊙	Add a colon.
ᶺᶺ	Add quotation marks.
ᵥ	Add an apostrophe.
≡	Capitalize.
╱	Make lower case.
ȣ	Delete.
¶	Make new paragraph.
◯	Check spelling.
⌐	Replace with this.
∿	Change order.
#	Insert space.
◡	Close up.

Australian and American Seasons

Did you know that seasons in Australia differ from seasons in the United States. It's true. unlike the U.S., Australia is in the southern part of the planet. Seasons are reversed there. what does this mean. In December, it's winter in the U.S., but it's summer in Australia. also, many parts of Australia have only two seasons, the wet and the dry seasons. in contrast, most of the U.S. has four seasons

Edit and Proofread Your Argument Paragraph

Now edit and proofread your work.

1. Use a checklist as you edit and proofread. Add things you are working on to the checklist.

2. Look to see which errors are marked most often. Jot down your top three trouble spots.

_____

_____

_____

Remember to Check	
☐	capitalization at the beginning of each sentence
☐	periods at the end of statements or commands
☐	question marks at the end of questions
☐	_____
☐	_____

3. Ask your teacher about ways to fix these errors, or see the Grammar Handbook.

Well-Organized Paragraph

What makes this well-organized paragraph a good model? Read the paragraph and answer the questions.

Buying a New Sari

by Uzma Patel

I need a new sari for next week's Diwali celebration. Diwali is very important to my family. My aunt used to send us saris from India. She designs them in her free time. Our neighborhood in Houston has lots of shops that sell saris. I can pick out my own at one of these shops. My favorite store is Khandwa Imports. They have a nice selection of saris. I think I'll get a yellow and blue one.

Feature Checklist

A well-organized paragraph

☐ has a topic sentence that states the main idea

☐ contains details or examples that tell more about the main idea

☐ presents all the ideas in the best order.

1. Does the topic sentence state the main idea?

   _____

   _____

   _____

2. Which details tell more about the paragraph's main idea?

   _____

   _____

   _____

   _____

3. Are there any details that do not go with the main idea?

   _____

   _____

   _____

   _____

4. Are the ideas presented in the best order?

   _____

   _____

   _____

Connect Main Idea and Details

Use each topic sentence to build a paragraph. Choose details that go with the main idea in the topic sentence. Add them to your paragraph. Rewrite the detail sentences in your own words if you need to.

Topic Sentence: Chicago has a large Polish population.

Details

• The population of the United States is about 300 million.	• There are more Poles in Chicago than any other city in the world outside Warsaw, Poland.
• The Polish community on the northwest side of Chicago is called "Polonia."	• Many immigrants moved to Chicago to escape the political problems in Poland.
• Large groups of Poles started immigrating to Chicago in 1850.	• A pierogi is a traditional Polish food.

_____

_____

_____

_____

_____

_____

_____

Topic Sentence: New Orleans still shows its French roots.

Details

• New Orleans has a large German community.	• Many people in New Orleans still speak French and are sometimes called Cajuns.
• The French founded the city in 1717 and controlled it for many years.	• The architecture in the French Quarter section of New Orleans is colonial French style.

_____

_____

_____

_____

_____

_____

_____

Plan and Write a Paragraph

Use pages 15–16 to plan and write a paragraph that describes what the word *home* means to you.

1. Take time to think about what the word *home* means. Jot these thoughts down.

_____

_____

_____

_____

2. Decide on your main idea. The main idea should sum up what *home* means to you.

_____

_____

3. To plan your paragraph, write down details that support your main idea.

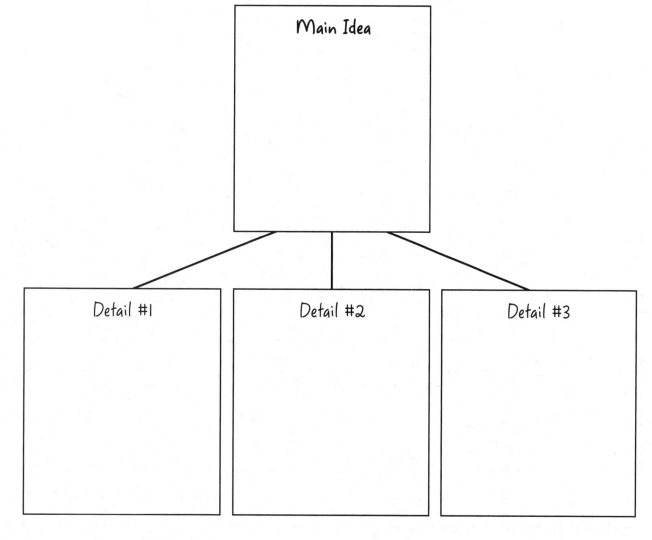

4. Use your graphic organizer on page 15 to write a paragraph. Start by using the main idea to form a topic sentence. Then, turn the details into sentences that support the main idea.

_____

_____

_____

_____

_____

_____

_____

_____

_____

_____

_____

_____

_____

_____

_____

_____

_____

_____

_____

_____

_____

_____

_____

_____

Revise a Paragraph

1. Evaluate this draft of a paragraph. What changes are needed?

_____

_____

_____

_____

_____

2. Revise the draft. Use revising marks to show your changes.

Revising

MARK	WHAT IT MEANS
∧	Insert something.
↶	Move to here.
⌃	Replace with this.
⸍	Take out.
¶	Make a new paragraph.

Little Persia

Many Iranian immigrants live in an area of Los Angeles known as Little Persia. Many came between the 1970s and the 1990s. As I walk through Little Persia, I love hearing bits of Persian conversation and music. My parents tell me that the sights and sounds and fragrances remind them of home.

There are dozens of food stores, restaurants, and bakeries there. One shop sells rose petal ice cream. I love its soft, sweet smell and taste. Ice cream is popular during the summer.

3. Now use the checklist to help you revise the draft of your paragraph on page 16. Use a clean sheet of paper.

Edit and Proofread

Mechanics Workout: Check Sentences and Paragraphs

Find and fix any errors in punctuation, capitalization, and indentation.

Editing and Proofreading Marks

Mark	Meaning
∧	Insert something.
∧	Add a comma.
∧	Add a semicolon.
⊙	Add a period.
⊙	Add a colon.
✓✓	Add quotation marks.
✓	Add an apostrophe.
≡	Capitalize.
/	Make lower case.
⌿	Delete.
¶	Make new paragraph.
◯	Check spelling.
⌒	Replace with this.
∿	Change order.
#	Insert space.
⌣	Close up.

Hooray for Bollywood

Watching Bollywood films makes Anjali happy, bollywood is a nickname for the Indian movie industry It's Based in Mumbai. These movies often have elaborate song-and-dance numbers.and unbelievable plots. Anjali knows they are a bit cheesy. But she still loves to watch, them with her friends. sometimes she spends the whole weekend watching them

Edit and Proofread Your Paragraph

Now edit and proofread your work.

1. Use a checklist as you edit and proofread. Add things you are working on to the checklist.

2. Look to see which errors are marked most often. Jot down your top three trouble spots.

Remember to Check

- ☐ capitalization
- ☐ correct punctuation marks
- ☐ indented paragraph
- ☐ _____
- ☐ _____

_____

_____

_____

3. Ask your teacher about ways to fix these mistakes, or check out the Grammar Handbook for information.

Sequence Paragraph

What makes this sequence paragraph a good model? Read it and answer the questions.

A Wet Day at the Pool

by Ramon Feliz

When Jim and Pam decided to go to the pool, they knew they would get wet. They didn't know they would get soaked! Like most July days, that Saturday was hot, and the sun was shining. The neighborhood swimming pool was crowded. It seemed everyone was trying to beat the heat. Jim and Pam enjoyed being submerged in the cool water. They took turns jumping off the diving platform. Both tried to see who could make the biggest splash. Suddenly, someone shouted, "Lightning!" Jim looked up and saw the sky rapidly turn dark. After that, the rain started to pour down. It was so heavy Jim could hardly see. Just then, the sky lit up with a bolt of lightning. Immediately, people started to panic. They jumped out of the pool and rushed to the clubhouse. Jim grabbed Pam by the arm and sprinted over to the snack stand canopy. Meanwhile, lifeguards were signaling to get everyone away from the pool. The rain continued for another half an hour. Jim and Pam stayed under the canopy until they could duck into the clubhouse. Eventually the rain stopped, but the dark clouds didn't go away. Jim and Pam decided to head home. They could not believe their beautiful day turned so ugly. Who knew the rain would be the one to make the biggest splash?

Feature Checklist

A good sequence paragraph

☐ has a topic sentence that states the main idea

☐ includes details that tell more about the main idea

☐ presents events in time order.

1. **What is the topic sentence? How does it introduce the main idea of the story?**

_____

_____

_____

_____

2. **What details tell more about the main idea?**

_____

_____

_____

_____

_____

3. **What words help signal, or show, the order in which the events happened?**

_____

_____

_____

_____

_____

Show the Sequence of Events

Read the events in the storyboard. Then, read the topic sentence on the line below. Complete the paragraph to tell the story. Use time-order words to show the sequence.

Who: Adrienne and Leslie
When and Where: morning, at a swim meet
What happens:

Beginning	**Middle**	**End**
Two girls are swimming hard in a tight race.	The finish is so close it needs to be reviewed by the official.	Adrienne loses. She is disappointed, but proud of her little sister, Leslie, for winning the race.

The swimming relay race came down to the last lap between Adrienne and Leslie.

_____

_____

_____

_____

_____

_____

_____

_____

_____

_____

_____

_____

_____

_____

_____

_____

Plan and Write a Sequence Paragraph

Use the following steps to write a sequence paragraph.

1. Decide on a main event. Sum up your main event in one sentence.

_____

_____

2. Brainstorm and organize details. Use the web below to list your events in order.

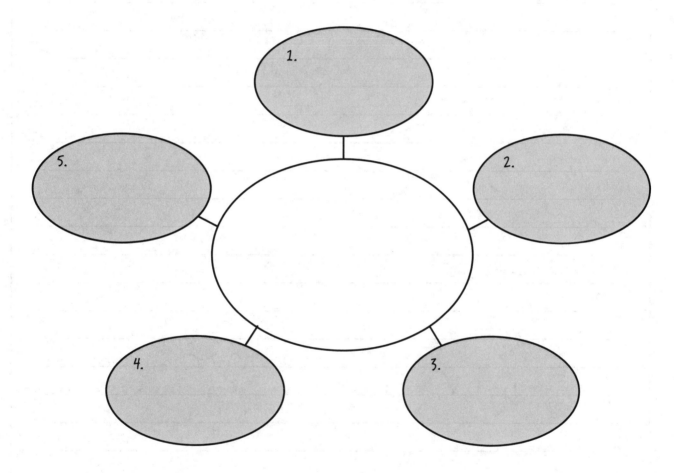

3. State the main idea of your paragraph in a topic sentence.

_____

_____

Use your plan on page 21 and follow these steps to write your sequence paragraph.

4. Add a few details that will help the reader know where and when the event takes place.

5. Tell your events in the order they happened. Use time-order words to help readers follow the story.

© National Geographic Learning, a part of Cengage Learning, Inc.

Revise a Sequence Paragraph

1. Use the checklist to evaluate this draft of a sequence paragraph. What changes are needed?

_____

_____

_____

_____

Revising Checklist

☐ Does your paragraph have a topic sentence that states the main idea?

☐ Did you include details that tell more about the main idea?

☐ Did you take out details that don't belong?

2. Revise the draft. Use revising marks to show your changes.

Revising

MARK	WHAT IT MEANS
∧	Insert something.
↶	Move to here.
⌐	Replace with this.
___	Take out.
¶	Make a new paragraph.

The Fishing Trip

Jesse and his dad went on their first fishing trip together. They got to the lake early in the morning. Jesse was tired! First, Jesse's dad showed him how to put worms on the fishing hook. The moist dirt was full of worms. Then, they cast their lines into the water. Jesse was glad to spend time with his dad. His dad had been planning the trip for weeks. Suddenly, something tugged on Jesse's fishing line! Jesse and his dad reeled the fish in together. Jesse felt great about catching his first fish.

3. Now use the checklist to help you revise the draft of your sequence paragraph on page 22. Use a clean sheet of paper.

Edit and Proofread

Grammar Workout: Check for Specific Nouns

Write a more specific noun to replace the underlined general noun in the sentence. You may replace a noun with more than one word.

1. Clark planned a canoeing trip with his <u>family</u>.

_____

2. The <u>river</u> was famous for its exciting waters.

_____

3. Clark hoped to see a rare <u>animal</u> that was known to live along the river.

_____

4. It would be cold, so Clark packed some <u>clothes</u>.

_____

5. He also packed extra <u>food</u> in case they got hungry.

_____

Spelling Workout: Check Plural Nouns

Fill in the blank with the correct plural form of the word in parentheses.

1. The Beatrice River has a few man-made _____ to camp on. **(beach)**

2. Clark's brother can start a campfire without using _____. **(match)**

3. The beach requires people to put their campfires out at night so the _____ don't cause a forest fire. **(flame)**

4. There are two supply _____ along the river. **(shop)**

5. The boys bought two _____ of crackers to eat along the way. **(box)**

6. Clark and his brother saw beautiful _____ on their way back to the river. **(bush)**

Edit and Proofread, continued

Mechanics Workout: Check Capitalization of Proper Nouns

Use proofreading marks to correct the capitalization errors in each sentence.

1. clark has canoed in many rivers in the united states.

2. Last year he canoed in the montress river in new Hampshire.

3. Clark's friend jim from tucson, arizona, suggested the river.

4. The river had a nice view of mount peterson and the roosevelt memorial bridge.

5. Next trip, Clark would like to canoe in lake michigan or another one of the Great lakes.

Check Grammar, Spelling, and Mechanics

Proofread the passage. Correct errors in spelling and capitalization. Replace general nouns with specific nouns.

Editing and Proofreading Marks	
∧	Insert something.
∧	Add a comma.
∧	Add a semicolon.
⊙	Add a period.
⊙	Add a colon.
ᵛ ᵛ	Add quotation marks.
ᵛ	Add an apostrophe.
≡	Capitalize.
/	Make lower case.
℘	Delete.
¶	Make new paragraph.
◯	Check spelling.
⤆	Replace with this.
∿	Change order.
#	Insert space.
◡	Close up.

When canoeing on the river, Clark daydreams. Sometimes he pretends he and his brother ben are cowboyes. They ride the waves like they are riding animals. Or clark thinks of himself as an explorer. He imagines he is with meriwether lewis and william clark floating down the missouri river. They see foxess along the shore. They even meet some people. They travel all the way to the beachs of the Pacific ocean! Clark never gets bored because he has so many thoughts and wishs to keep him excited.

Edit and Proofread Your Sequence Paragraph

Now edit and proofread your work.

1. Use a checklist as you edit and proofread. Add things you are working on to the checklist.

2. Look to see which errors are marked most often. Jot down your top three trouble spots.

_____

_____

_____

3. Ask your teacher about ways to fix these mistakes, or check out the Grammar Handbook for information.

Focus on Spelling

Improve your spelling by following these steps.

1. Create a personal spelling list. Record words that you misspelled and look up correct spelling in the dictionary.

2. Pick twelve words. Write each word four times. First, write it in all lowercase letters. Next, write it in all capital letters. After that, write the vowels in lowercase and the consonants in uppercase. Last, write the word using fancy letters that you create on your own. For example, your letters can be curly or tall or skinny.

3. Work with a partner to play **I'm Thinking of a Spelling Word**. Take turns giving each other clues. Some clues might be _I'm thinking of a word that rhymes with . . . , I'm thinking of a word that begins with . . . ,_ or _I'm thinking of a word that means . . ._ For each clue, the answer should include the word and its spelling.

4. Play a scrambled-letter game with a partner. Take each other's spelling words and write them in scrambled form. See who can unscramble all the words first.

5. Use an audio recorder and record your words and their spelling. Then listen to your tape, checking to see that you spelled each word correctly.

Collect Ideas

1. Check out the idea file on this page and add some ideas of your own.

My friends drink a lot of water!

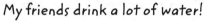

Quotations and Ideas

"Anyone who can solve the problems of water will be worthy of two Nobel prizes — one for peace and one for science."

—John F. Kennedy

"The day, water, sun, moon, night — I do not have to purchase these things with money."

—Roman poet Titus Maccius Plautus

_____

_____

_____

_____

_____

_____

_____

_____

Topics that Interest Me

1. Humans and animals need water to survive.

2. You can get fresh water in many places.

3. It can be bought in a store or found in nature.

Collect Ideas, continued

Find Your Truth

2. Write a truth for each photograph. Tell what you believe is true about the situation.

A.

_____

_____

_____

B.

_____

_____

_____

C.

_____

_____

_____

D.

_____

_____

_____

Choose Your Topic

1. **Choose a topic that involves water. Use this graphic to narrow your topic. Make it specific enough to cover in a couple of pages.**

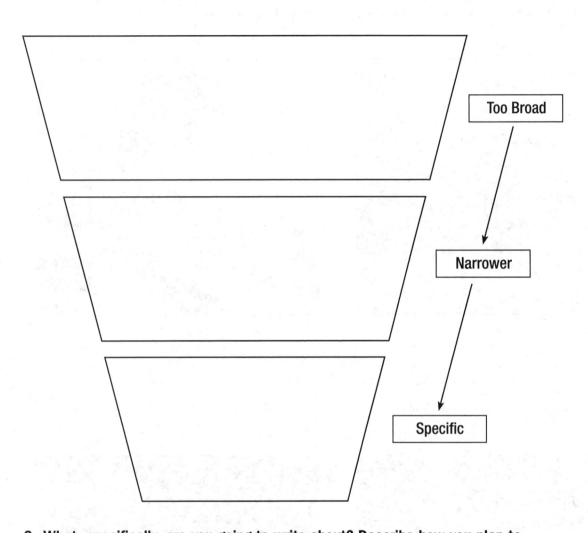

Too Broad

Narrower

Specific

2. **What, specifically, are you going to write about? Describe how you plan to approach the topic.**

_____

_____

_____

_____

_____

_____

_____

_____

_____

_____

Choose Your Audience

Complete the chart. Write down the tone and give an example of the language that should be used when writing an e-mail to each audience.

AUDIENCE	TONE	LANGUAGE
your best friend or someone your age		
an older relative		
your teacher		
someone you do not know		

Choose Your Purpose

1. **What you hope to accomplish with your writing is your purpose. Look at the chart below. Add examples from your own writing or reading experience for each purpose listed.**

If You Want Your Audience to. . .	Your purpose is. . .	Examples?
· learn something new · understand something better	to inform or explain	_____ _____ _____ _____
· laugh · feel deep emotion · enjoy reading your work	to narrate	_____ _____ _____ _____
· know how you think · believe something · do something · take action on an important issue	to argue	_____ _____ _____ _____

2. **Study the photo. Choose a purpose for writing about it. Write a few sentences explaining how you might achieve your purpose.**

Purpose: _____

_____

_____

_____

Sentences: _____

_____

_____

Choose a Structure

Study the FATP Chart and notes. Organize the information in different ways.

FATP Chart

Form: _informative paragraph_

Audience: _classmates_

Topic: _Hot Springs National Park in Arkansas_

Purpose: _to explain how the hot springs in the national park are created_

Hot Springs National Park

• A hot spring is filled by heated groundwater that comes to the surface.

• The hot springs in Hot Springs National Park are created by heat from the Earth called geothermal heat.

• The water is heated by the rocks in the Earth's core.

• The water temperature in the springs reaches about 143°F.

• Groundwater from springs sinks deep into the Earth's core.

source: http://www.nps.gov/hosp/index.htm

1. To explain what happened, list the ideas in the order in which they occur.

_____

_____

_____

_____

_____

_____

2. Organize the ideas to make a comparison. Complete the left half of the chart.

Hot Springs	Other Bodies of Water
_____	The water temperature is typically close to the air temperature of the area.
_____	The water is heated by the sun.
_____	Other bodies of water are filled by rain, melted glaciers, or other methods.
_____	_____
_____	_____

Choose a Structure, continued

3. **What water-related topic will you write about?
   Complete the FATP Chart. Then complete a
   graphic organizer to organize your ideas. Does the
   organizer go well with your purpose and your form?**

FATP Chart

Form: _____

Audience: _____

Topic: _____

_____

Purpose: _____

_____

Draft

Use your plan from page 34 to write the first draft of your paragraphs.

Drafting Checklist

☐ The message is clear, and the writing stays on topic.

☐ Ideas are organized in an effective order.

☐ The purpose is clear.

☐ The form and tone are appropriate for the intended audience.

_____
_____
_____
_____
_____
_____
_____
_____
_____
_____
_____
_____
_____
_____
_____
_____
_____
_____
_____
_____
_____
_____
_____
_____

Revise: Gather Ideas

Use pages 37–38 to think about your writing, get feedback, and plan what changes you'll make to your paper.

Evaluate for Audience and Purpose

1. Read the paragraph below aloud. Evaluate the paragraph for audience and a purpose. Use the boxes to write down any thoughts or concerns.

From Salty to Fresh
by Holly Kayse

What if the water in your school's drinking fountain came from the ocean? That would be gross. Water from the ocean is too salty to drink. But did you know there are ways to turn salt water into fresh water? The process is called desalination. There are many methods of desalination. One way is to heat the water until it boils. The water vapors, which don't contain salt, are collected for drinking water. There are also high-tech methods. These include reverse osmosis and electrodialysis. They use either pressure or electricity to separate salt molecules from the water. During the last 50 years, desalination has become very popular. It is especially useful to people living in dry areas like the Middle East. This region produces about 75 percent of the world's desalinated water. The United States produces 10 percent. So maybe your drinking water is from the ocean. Minus the salt, of course!

2. Now read your own work and evaluate it for audience and purpose.

3. Read your paper to yourself. What parts sound good to you? What parts need more work? Why? _____

_____

_____

_____

4. Read your paper aloud to one peer and one adult. Ask them how you can improve your draft. Write down any answers you can use to revise your paper.

_____

_____

_____

5. Have a peer conference. Use the feedback you get to answer these questions:

What's the best thing about your writing?

_____

_____

What do you need to work on to improve your writing?

_____

_____

What other changes did your readers suggest?

_____

_____

6. Now you're ready to decide how you will revise your paper. Describe the changes you plan to make.

_____

_____

_____

_____

_____

7. Apply those changes to your explanatory paragraphs.

Revision in Action

1. Use the checklist to evaluate this draft of an explanatory paragraph. What changes are needed?

_____

_____

_____

_____

_____

Revising Checklist

- ☐ Does the form of your draft match your purpose for writing?
- ☐ Does each paragraph include a main idea?
- ☐ Do the ideas flow smoothly? Do you need to add transitions?
- ☐ Do any of the parts need more detail or explanation?

2. Revise this draft. If you need to, do research to find a few details to add.

Revising

MARK	WHAT IT MEANS
∧	Insert something.
↶	Move to here.
∧—	Replace with this.
⌿	Take out.
¶	Make a new paragraph.

Exploring the Parker Dam

The Parker Dam is on the border between Arizona and California. The dam was built a long time ago. It is famous for its size. It also provides important services. The dam separates Lake Havasu from the Colorado River. It can store 211 billion gallons of water. Most of it is under water, making it the deepest dam in the world. The dam provides water to Southern California. Parker Dam is large, but it is not the largest dam in the world. It produces power for communities in the Southwest.

3. Now use the checklist to help you revise the draft of your paper on pages 35–36. Use a clean sheet of paper.

Edit and Proofread

Tools: The Dictionary

Edit and proofread the passage. Use the dictionary excerpt at the bottom of the page to check the spelling and meaning of words you're not sure of.

It was hot Thursday! It would have been excellently if we didn't have to be in school. Ms. Smith had the windows open in class, but it was still excedingly hot. At lunchtime, everyone had a cold drink excep me. So, I made an eschange with Sam. I gave him my cookie, and he gave me his bottle of water.

---

exceeding • excommunicate 330

production⟩. EXCEL implies preeminence in achievement or quality ⟨*excelling* in athletics⟩. SURPASS suggests superiority in quality, merit, or skill ⟨the book *surpassed* our expectations⟩. TRANSCEND implies a rising or extending notably above or beyond ordinary limits ⟨*transcended* the values of their culture⟩.

ex·ceed·ing \ik-ˈsēd-ing\ *adj* : exceptional in amount, quality, or degree ⟨*exceeding* darkness⟩

ex·ceed·ing·ly \ik-ˈsēd-ing-lē\ *also* **exceeding** *adv* : to an extreme degree ⟨an *exceedingly* fine job⟩

ex·cel \ik-ˈsel\ *vb* **ex·celled; ex·cel·ling** : to be superior : surpass in accomplishment or achievement ⟨*excels* in mathematics⟩ ⟨*excelled* her classmates⟩ [Latin *excellere*, from *ex-* + *-cellere* "to rise, project"] **synonyms** see EXCEED

ex·cel·lence \ˈek-sə-ləns, -sləns\ *n* **1** : the quality of being excellent **2** : an excellent or valuable quality : VIRTUE **3** : EXCELLENCY 2

ex·cel·len·cy \-sə-lən-sē, -slən-\ *n, pl* **-cies** **1** : outstanding or valuable quality — usually used in plural **2** — used as a form of address for a high dignitary of state (as a foreign ambassador) or church (as a Roman Catholic bishop) ⟨Your *Excellency*⟩

ex·cel·lent \ˈek-sə-lənt\ *adj* : very good of its kind : FIRST-CLASS — **ex·cel·lent·ly** *adv*

ex·cel·si·or \ik-ˈsel-sē-ər\ *n* : fine curled wood shavings used especially for packing fragile items [trade name, from Latin, "higher," from *excelsus* "high," from *excellere* "to excel"]

¹except *also* **ex·cept·ing** *prep* : with the exclusion or exception of ⟨everybody *except* you⟩ ⟨open daily *except* Sundays⟩

²ex·cept \ik-ˈsept\ *vt* : to take or leave out from a number or a whole : EXCLUDE, OMIT [Medieval French *excepter*, from Latin *exceptare*, from *excipere* "to take out, except," from *ex-* + *capere* "to take"]

³except *also* **excepting** *conj* **1** : UNLESS ⟨*except* you repent⟩ **2** : with this exception, namely ⟨was inaccessible *except* by boat⟩ **3** : ³ONLY 2 ⟨I would go *except* it's too far⟩

except for *prep* : with the exception of : but for ⟨all A's *except for* a B in Latin⟩

ex·cep·tion \ik-ˈsep-shən\ *n* **1** : the act of excepting : EXCLUSION **2** : one that is excepted; *esp* : a case where a rule does not apply ⟨we'll make an *exception* this time⟩ **3** : an objection or a ground for objection ⟨took *exception* to the remark⟩

ex·cep·tion·able \ik-ˈsep-shə-nə-bəl, -shnə-\ *adj* : likely to cause objection : OBJECTIONABLE — **ex·cep·tion·ably** \-blē\ *adv*

ex·cep·tion·al \ik-ˈsep-shnəl, -shən-l\ *adj* **1** : forming an exception : UNUSUAL ⟨an *exceptional* number of rainy days⟩ **2**

er **5** : a place where things or services are exchanged: as **a** : an organized market or center for trading in securities or commodities ⟨stock *exchange*⟩ **b** : a central office in which telephone lines are connected to permit communication

²exchange *vt* **1 a** : to give in exchange : TRADE, SWAP **b** : to replace by other merchandise ⟨*exchange* this shirt for one in a larger size⟩ **2** : to part with for a substitute ⟨*exchange* future security for immediate pleasure⟩ — **ex·change·able** \-ə-bəl\ *adj* — **ex·chang·er** *n*

exchange rate *n* : the ratio at which the principal units of two currencies may be traded

exchange student *n* : a student from one country received into a school in another country in exchange for one sent to a school in the home country of the first student

ex·che·quer \ˈeks-ˌchek-ər, iks-ˈ\ *n* **1** : the department of the British government concerned with the receipt and care of the national revenue **2** : TREASURY; *esp* : a national or royal treasury **3** : money available : FUNDS [Medieval French *escheker* "chessboard, counting table, exchequer," from *eschec* "check"]

¹ex·cise \ˈek-ˌsīz, -ˌsīs\ *n* : an internal tax levied on the manufacture, sale, or consumption of a commodity within a country [obsolete Dutch *excijs*]

²ex·cise \ek-ˈsīz\ *vt* : to remove by cutting out ⟨*excise* a tumor⟩ [Latin *excisus*, past participle of *excidere* "to excise," from *ex-* + *caedere* "to cut"] — **ex·ci·sion** \-ˈsizh-ən\ *n*

ex·cit·able \ik-ˈsīt-ə-bəl\ *adj* : readily roused into action or an active state; *esp* : capable of activation by and reaction to stimuli — **ex·cit·abil·i·ty** \-ˌsīt-ə-ˈbil-ət-ē\ *n*

ex·ci·ta·tion \ˌek-ˌsī-ˈtā-shən, ˌek-sə-\ *n* : EXCITEMENT; *esp* : the activity or change in condition resulting from stimulation of an individual, organ, tissue, or cell

ex·cit·a·to·ry \ik-ˈsīt-ə-ˌtōr-ē, -ˌtȯr-\ *adj* : tending to produce or marked by usually physiological excitation

ex·cite \ik-ˈsīt\ *vt* **1 a** : to call to activity **b** : to rouse to an emotional response **c** : to arouse (as an emotional response) by appropriate stimuli **2 a** : ENERGIZE **b** : to produce a magnetic field in **3** : to increase the activity of (as nervous tissue) **4** : to raise (as an atom) to a higher energy level [Medieval French *exciter*, from Latin *excitare*, from *ex-* + *citare* "to rouse"] **synonyms** see PROVOKE — **ex·cit·er** \-ˈsīt-ər\ *n*

ex·cit·ed \-ˈsīt-əd\ *adj* : having or showing strong feeling : worked up ⟨*excited* about the trip⟩ — **ex·cit·ed·ly** *adv*

ex·cite·ment \ik-ˈsīt-mənt\ *n* **1** : the act of exciting : the state of being excited **2** : something that excites

ex·cit·ing \-ˈsīt-ing\ *adj* : causing excitement : STIRRING ⟨*excit-*

Edit and Proofread, continued

Tools: Personal Checklists

A. Use this page to create your own personalized checklist of mistakes to watch out for.

1. Look back through your old papers to see which editing and proofreading errors are marked most frequently. Jot down your top five trouble spots.

_____

_____

_____

_____

_____

2. Talk with your teacher about ways to fix these mistakes, or check out the Grammar Handbook for tips.

3. Now, create your personal checklist. List your most common mistakes and how you can fix them.

My Editing Checklist

B. Find and fix any grammar, spelling, punctuation, and capitalization errors.
   Use the proofreader's marks on page 43.

Reversed River

During the 1800s, the Chicago River was an important body of water for for industy in Chicago. The River connected to many waterways. Most importantly, it conected the city too the Mississippi River. This allowed companies to ship goods to ports along the rivre. It also allowed good tobe imported. This was a central system for trade in the midwest. Many lumberyards, and meatpacking plants were built along the river. The companies used the river fro transporting goods. However they also used it for dumping sewage.

By 1870, the Chicago river was poluted. The polluted water flowed into Lake Michigan. This contaminated the city's fresh water. City officials new something had to be done. What did they do. They planned to reverse the river's flow. Engineers built a canal. It forced water to flow away from lake Michigan a nd into the Illinois Waterway. The project was finished in 1900. It is one of the greatestt achievements in engineering. Today, the Chicago River is still an active waterway. It's used by both barges and boates. Step have been taken to improve the water's quality. Still, the water turns green once a year. The city dies it green every St. Patrick's day.

© National Geographic Learning, a part of Cengage Learning, Inc.

Edit and Proofread, continued

Editing and Proofreading Marks

Mark	Meaning	Example
∧	Insert something.	This lake is beautᵢful.
∧	Add a comma.	I love to fish but I can't do it often.
∧	Add a semicolon.	I've never seen the Pacific Ocean I've heard it is amazing.
⊙	Add a period.	I love going to the beach
⊙	Add a colon.	The tide comes in at 7:30.
ᵛ ᵛ	Add quotation marks.	She yelled, What a view!
ᵛ	Add an apostrophe.	Anns pool is never clean.
≡	Capitalize.	It barely rains in the mojave desert.
/	Make lowercase.	I usually sit under Trees for shade.
ℐ	Delete, take something out.	My friend lives on an islands.
¶	Make new paragraph.	"I just saw a salmon!" I shouted. ¶"Where?" he asked.
◯	Spell out.	My mom has been to the (U.S.)
⌐∧	Replace with this.	His best friend is a ᵈᵒᵍ cat.
∼	Change order of letters or words.	My aunt's garden is really nojie, but it takes a (time long) to water.
#	Insert space.	Whales are mammals that live in the ocean.
◡	Close up, no space here.	I went to the aquarium to day.

C. Use the editing and proofreading marks on page 43 to edit this passage.

Clean Water

Water must be treated before it is safe to drink? Water comes from the ground, lakes and rivers. It is not alwys safe to drink. So, all water goes to water purification plants. These plants remvoe chemicals in water so it is safe to drink. This is called Filtering. After the water is filtered, it is made available to everyone. We would get sick from drinking dirty water with out this process.

Every manjor area has a filtration plant. The largest water filtration plant in the world is the Jardine Water Plant. It is in chicago, IL. It takes water from lake Michigan. It filters nearly one billion gallons of wa ter everyday. That's enough water to fill an Olympic-sized swimming pol every minute! This plant provides clean water to millions of people

Edit and Proofread, continued

D. Answer questions 1 and 2.

1. How many times do you usually proofread your work before it is finished?

_____

_____

2. Who do you know that is a good proofreader? Why do you think he or she is good at proofreading?

_____

_____

E. Read the questions about how you edit and proofread your papers. Circle the numbers that show how often you do these things.

How often do you . . .	Never	Rarely	Sometimes	Often
use an editing checklist?	1	2	3	4
mark errors and possible errors?	1	2	3	4
check in reference materials (dictionary, grammar book, style manual)?	1	2	3	4
correct grammar errors?	1	2	3	4
correct usage errors?	1	2	3	4
correct punctuation errors?	1	2	3	4
correct capitalization errors?	1	2	3	4
spelling errors?	1	2	3	4
list your most common types of errors to check for them in the future?	1	2	3	4

Editing and Proofreading in Action

Grammar Workout: Check Subject-Verb Agreement

Complete each sentence. Write the correct form of the verb.

1. Jamal and his brother _____ in their boat.
(sit/sits)

2. They both _____ their fishing lines into the water.
(drop/drops)

3. Jamal _____ his brother to stop rocking the boat.
(tell/tells)

4. The schools of fish _____ a boat is around if they _____ the
(know/knows) (see/sees)
water ripple.

5. Jamal's brother _____ excited when he _____ a tug on his
(get/gets) (feel/feels)
fishing line.

6. Suddenly, a big fish _____ into the boat!
(jump/jumps)

Spelling Workout: Check Plural Nouns

Fill in the blank with the correct plural form of the word in parentheses.

1. There was a group of _____ having a picnic next to the lake. **(lady)**

2. Some _____ buzzed around their food. **(fly)**

3. There were also some children playing with their _____ a few feet away.
(toy)

4. A lady walked over and gave the children some chocolate _____. **(candy)**

5. The _____ of sun shone off the water and reflected onto the children's
smiling faces. **(ray)**

6. I took a picture of one of the _____ enjoying his piece of candy. **(boy)**

7. It's true: one picture can tell a million _____. **(story)**

Editing and Proofreading in Action, continued

Mechanics Workout: Check Abbreviations

Use proofreading marks to make as many abbreviations as possible in each sentence.

1. Natural spring water flows down from Mount Fuji.

2. Mister Carlson will only drink bottled water that comes from this region.

3. He buys it from the drug store off Waverly Avenue in Fort George.

4. Doctor Jackson says the water is like any other water.

5. Mr. Carlson even got his dad, Senator Harold Carlson Sr., to drink the water.

Check Grammar, Spelling, and Mechanics

Proofread the passage. Check the spelling and subject-verb agreement. Use as many abbreviations as you can.

Editing and Proofreading Marks	
∧	Insert something.
⩓	Add a comma.
⩞	Add a semicolon.
⊙	Add a period.
⊙	Add a colon.
ⱽ ⱽ	Add quotation marks.
ⱽ	Add an apostrophe.
≡	Capitalize.
/	Make lower case.
℘	Delete.
¶	Make new paragraph.
◯	Check spelling.
⌒	Replace with this.
∾	Change order.
#	Insert space.
◡	Close up.

Dear Mister Akiko,

I really enjoy the bottled water that the Fuji Springs Company make. I've traveled to many citys to get your product. Most people thinks I'm crazy. I've tried many different remedys to cure my aching back. Your water is the only thing that help it. My physician, Doctor Steele, think it was just a coincidence. In a few daies, I'm going to fly from the United States to Japan. I would like to visit one of your factorys. Maybe I can drink straight from the spring.

Sincerely,

Harold Carlson, Jr.

Mister Harold Carlson, Junior

Edit and Proofread Your Paragraphs

Now edit and proofread your work.

Remember to Check

- ☐ subject-verb agreement
- ☐ spelling of plural nouns
- ☐ use of abbreviations
- ☐ _____
- ☐ _____

1. Use a checklist as you edit and proofread. Add things you are working on to the checklist.

2. Look to see which errors are marked most often. Jot down your top three trouble spots.

_____

_____

_____

3. Ask your teacher about ways to fix these mistakes, or check out the Grammar Handbook for information.

Focus on Spelling

Improve your spelling by following these steps.

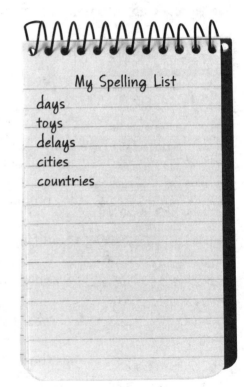

1. Create a personal spelling list. Record words that you misspelled. Look up the correct spelling in the dictionary and add these words to **My Spelling List**.

2. Pick twelve words. Make a colorful display of the words. Get a sheet of chart paper. Write each word three times in a different color.

3. Work with a partner to play **Spelling Tic-Tac-Toe**. Draw a tic-tac-toe board. Take turns asking each other to spell words. When a player spells a word correctly, that player gets to mark an X or an O on the game board.

4. Write the letters for each word on separate squares of paper. Attach the letters for each word to each other with a paper clip. Unscramble the letters to spell each of your words.

5. Invent your own memory strategy for difficult words. Think of a good way to remember *why* letters appear or not in a word. For example:

Word	Explanation
dessert	"It has two s's for <u>s</u>weet <u>s</u>tuff!"

Publish, Share, and Reflect

Publish and Share Your Paragraphs

**Check the final formats you used to publish your paragraphs.
Then answer the following questions.**

Publishing	
What was the final format of your project?	**How did you share your project?**
☐ Wrote it neatly by hand	☐ Shared it with a large group
☐ Typed it on a computer	☐ Shared it with a small group

1. Whether you published it by hand or on the computer, what did you do to dress up your final project?

_____

_____

_____

_____

_____

2. How did you share your work? What did you learn through sharing your work?

_____

_____

_____

_____

_____

_____

_____

_____

_____

_____

_____

_____

Reflect on Your Paragraphs

Read your paragraphs. Then answer questions 1–6.

1. What do you like best about your work? _____

_____

_____

2. What did you do well? _____

_____

_____

3. What could you improve about your work? _____

_____

_____

_____

4. How will you choose to share your work? _____

_____

_____

5. What can you do to make your work right for your audience? _____

_____

_____

6. Will you add your paragraphs to your Writing Portfolio? Explain your decision.

❑ Yes, I will add this to my Writing Portfolio.

_____

_____

❑ No, I will not add this to my Writing Portfolio.

_____

_____

Friendly Letter

What makes this letter a good model?
Read it and answer the questions.

November 12, 2014

Dear Jaycee,

How are you doing? You're lucky that your family moved to New York. You escaped the flood! It started raining early last week and kept raining for three days straight! I was starting to forget what the sun looked like.

Luckily, there was a flood warning. We were told to evacuate the area. My parents and I live near the ocean. So we moved in with my grandma. She lives far away from the water, where it's safer.

The rain got so heavy that some roads were closed off. School was cancelled for two days. Then it finally stopped raining, but we couldn't move back into our house. We were lucky. Our house was flooded, but not destroyed. There was a lot of damage to the inside. It will be a few months before we can move back home.

It was quite an adventure! I can't wait until the rainy season is over. I'm looking forward to visiting you this summer!

Your friend,
Brenna

Feature Checklist

A good friendly letter

☐ begins with the date in the upper right corner

☐ includes a greeting

☐ uses an informal tone to tell about personal things

☐ asks about your friend's life

☐ includes a closing before the signature.

1. How does Brenna start her letter?

_____

_____

_____

2. How do you know Brenna is writing to a friend?

_____

_____

_____

3. What does Brenna share about her life?

_____

_____

_____

_____

4. How does Brenna's letter end?

_____

_____

_____

_____

_____

_____

Prewrite

Use pages 52–53 to plan your friendly letter.

1. Choose One Experience to Write About

For a short friendly letter, it's best to focus on just one experience. Think about fun things you've done lately and pick one to write about.

Ideas

2. Think About Your Audience and Purpose

Choose your details based on what will interest your audience. Your purpose will also determine how you write. Do you want to just give information, or do you want to entertain the reader, too?

Fill out an FATP Chart to help you stay focused.

FATP Chart

Form: _____

Audience: _____

Topic: _____

_____

Purpose: _____

_____

© National Geographic Learning, a part of Cengage Learning, Inc.

Prewrite, continued

3. Organize Your Main Ideas and Details

Before you start writing, organize your ideas. Use a graphic organizer like the one below to put your topic sentence and details in order.

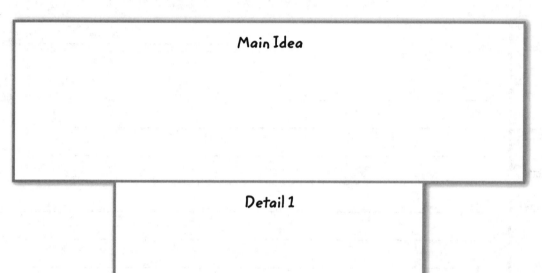

Main Idea

Detail 1

Detail 2

Detail 3

Draft a Friendly Letter

Use your plan from pages 52–53 to write the first draft of your letter.

Drafting Checklist

- [ ] Begin with the date in the upper right corner.
- [ ] Include a greeting.
- [ ] Use an informal tone to tell about what's going on in your life.
- [ ] Keep the details organized and flowing smoothly. Start with a topic sentence and then add details.
- [ ] Ask about your friend's life.
- [ ] Include a closing before your signature.

_____

_____

_____

_____

_____

_____

_____

_____

_____

_____

_____

_____

_____

_____

_____

_____

_____

_____

_____

Revise a Friendly Letter

1. Evaluate this draft of a friendly letter. What changes are needed?

_____

_____

_____

_____

_____

2. Revise the draft. Use revising marks to show your changes.

Revising

MARK	WHAT IT MEANS
∧	Insert something.
↶	Move to here.
↶	Replace with this.
⟋	Take out.
¶	Make a new paragraph.

September 14, 2014

Dear Uncle Max,

Thanks for coming to visit us ! I hope you had as much fun as we did.

Practically everyone couldn't stop talking about you. You were so nice to come to my class while you were here. Your experiences as a volcanologist were awesome!

Mom says we might be planning a trip to Hawaii soon. You'll have to come with us. Speaking of volcanoes, have you ever been to Hawaii? Then we could see a real volcano!

Mandy

3. Now use the checklist to help you revise the draft of your friendly letter on page 54. Use a clean sheet of paper.

Edit and Proofread

Grammar Workout: Check Pronouns

Complete each sentence. Use the correct pronoun.

1. My aunt looked out the window. _____ saw smoke coming from the volcano.

2. _____ looked like a dark rain cloud.

3. The first thing _____ did was pick up her sons from school.

4. _____ were scared by the loud noise.

5. _____ scared all the kids in their class.

6. Their teacher, Mr. Samuels, said _____ had never heard such a loud noise.

Spelling Workout: Check Compound Words

Write the correct form of the compound word in each sentence.

1. Mauna Loa is the _____ volcano on the island.
   (bestknown/best-known)

2. Jess and I were playing _____ when we heard the eruption.
   (softball/soft ball)

3. My sister was on the _____ when she heard it.
   (playground/play ground)

4. The blast caused windows in the _____ to break.
   (postoffice/post office)

5. My _____ heard the noise and was terrified.
   (grand mother/grandmother)

6. Everyone on the island is _____ now. **(all right/allright)**

Edit and Proofread, continued

Mechanics Workout: Check Commas and Capitalization

Check the greeting, closing, and date in the letter. Fix the errors.

Editing and Proofreading Marks	
∧	Insert something.
⋏	Add a comma.
⋏	Add a semicolon.
⊙	Add a period.
⊙	Add a colon.
ᵛᵛ	Add quotation marks.
ᵛ	Add an apostrophe.
≡	Capitalize.
/	Make lower case.
ℰ	Delete.
¶	Make new paragraph.
⬯	Check spelling.
⌒	Replace with this.
∿	Change order.
#	Insert space.
⌣	Close up.

july 27 2014

Dear mom

   Guess what happened at Grandma's? A volcano erupted.

It made a big boom. She was scared, but we are okay. It will

take the town some time to clean up the mess, though!

love

Eric

Check Grammar, Spelling, and Mechanics

Fix errors with pronouns, compound words, capitalization, and commas.

June 27 2014

dear Abby,

   How are you? Is your class studying volcanoes yet? We are. We built a

volcano in our class-room. My teacher, Mr. Ito, told us about the bestknown

eruption in the U.S. They said it was in Washington on may 18, 1980. She

was terrible. People living 250 miles away had ashes in their yards and on their

houses. They blocked the sunlight. I'm glad I don't live next to a volcano!

your friend

Stefanie

Edit and Proofread Your Friendly Letter

Now edit and proofread your work.

1. Use the checklist as you edit and proofread.
   Add things you are working on to the checklist.

2. Look to see which errors are marked most often.
   Jot down your top three trouble spots.

_____

_____

3. Ask your teacher about ways to fix these mistakes,
   or check out the Grammar Handbook for information.

Focus on Spelling

Improve your spelling by following these steps.

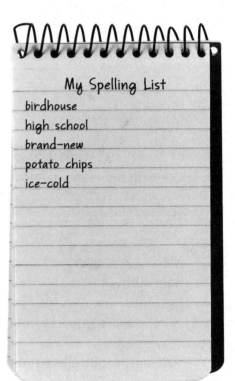

My Spelling List
birdhouse
high school
brand-new
potato chips
ice-cold

1. Create a personal spelling list. Record words that you
   misspelled. Look up the correct spelling in the dictionary
   and add the words to **My Spelling List**.

2. Pick twelve words. Make each word look interesting and
   special by tracing it five times. Write the word in one
   color. Then trace it four more times in four different
   colors. Say each letter to yourself as you trace it.

3. Play **Spelling Catch** with a partner. Pitch words to each
   other by saying, "Here's the pitch. The word is …" Take
   turns. The first "batter" to spell ten words correctly wins.

4. Write each spelling word three times. First, just write the
   word. Second, write it and circle the consonants. Third,
   write it and circle the vowels.

5. Play **Memory** to help you remember your words. Write each spelling word on
   two different index cards. Mix up the cards and place them face down. Turn
   the cards over two at a time. Your goal is to find the matching cards. Say and
   spell the words on the cards you turn over. If you make a match, remove those
   cards from the game. You've won when you've removed all the cards.

Personal Narrative

**What makes this personal narrative a good model?
Read the narrative and answer the questions.**

Too Much Excitement
by Pedro Martinez

My sister and I looked forward to our summer vacation this year. It was our reward for working hard and getting good grades during the spring semester. We hoped it would be an exciting vacation, and it was. One of the days was just a little too exciting, though!

We were visiting our aunt and uncle in Florida for the first time. They live in a big house in a beautiful area along the coast. They took us to an aquarium, a museum, a mall, and a couple of amusement parks. We saw a movie and two musical theater shows. We walked downtown, and we visited the beach a few times. That was my favorite place. Every day we did something new and interesting.

One day the four of us were walking along the beach with my aunt's German shepherd, Kemoo. The white sand was soft and warm. It was peaceful and sunny, a perfect day except for some clouds in the sky.

Suddenly Kemoo began to run in circles and bark wildly. I looked up. The sky was getting dark quickly. It was almost black. It began to get windy, too. We all got in the car and drove the short distance to my aunt and uncle's home.

Feature Checklist

A good personal narrative

- ☐ has a beginning, a middle, and an end
- ☐ includes real events, people, and places
- ☐ uses specific details that let the reader "see and feel" what's happening
- ☐ expresses the writer's feelings.

1. How does the beginning get the readers' attention? What does it tell?

_____

_____

_____

_____

2. How can you tell that the places, events, and people are real?

_____

_____

_____

_____

_____

3. What details let the reader "see and feel" what's happening?

_____

_____

_____

_____

_____

By the time we got there, it was raining. We rushed inside. Soon, the rain poured down. It sounded like rocks were hitting the roof and walls. The wind howled—I thought it would blow the house down! I had never been so frightened in all my life! It was a hurricane. The storm had not been forecast to hit that area, but it had changed direction.

The wind and rain continued through the long night. The power went out, so we went to bed early. But the storm was loud, and I was scared, so I couldn't sleep at all.

The next morning, the skies cleared. We were lucky. The main part of the hurricane did not hit the area we were in. Some buildings and trees were damaged, but it could have been much worse. No one was badly hurt.

My uncle explained: "Sometimes a hurricane changes its course, or direction. I should have paid closer attention to the latest weather reports. We could have been better prepared for this."

I guess Florida isn't perfect, after all. I guess no place is completely safe. In California, where I live, we worry about earthquakes and wildfires. In other areas, people worry about floods, tornadoes, or snowstorms.

Still, my sister and I had fun during our vacation. I'm sure we'll never forget it! I'm sure I'll visit Florida again, too, because I love everything about it. Well, *almost* everything!

4. **What other details let the reader "see and feel" what's happening?**

_____

_____

_____

_____

_____

5. **What helps you understand how the writer is feeling?**

_____

_____

_____

_____

_____

_____

_____

_____

6. **What is good about the ending?**

_____

_____

_____

_____

_____

© National Geographic Learning, a part of Cengage Learning, Inc.

Organization

Read each personal narrative. Use the rubric on page 62 to score each narrative for organization. Explain your scores.

Writing Sample 1

Evacuation

I got up to answer the knock at the door. It was a sheriff's deputy. "Are your parents home?" he asked.

"No, they're at work," I answered. I was home alone on a stormy evening with my kid sister, Janine.

"You need to evacuate now," the deputy said. "The waters are rising fast. It's not safe for you to stay here. Do you have a car? Can you drive?"

"Yes, I can drive. Okay, I'll go," I said, and I closed the door. Questions ran through my mind: *What about all of our stuff? What should I bring? If I leave, will looters try to break in? Where should I go?*

I grabbed Janine and got into my truck. As I warmed up the engine, I called my mom on my cell phone to let her know what was happening.

Score	1	2	3	4

_____
_____
_____
_____
_____
_____
_____
_____

Writing Sample 2

Stuck

This can't be happening, I thought. I was in my truck, stuck in a stream, surrounded by rising flood water.

About an hour before, a sheriff's deputy came to my house and advised me to evacuate. I decided to stay home instead. But finally I had to go.

I saw the water flowing over that road. It was only about six inches deep. I thought I could drive through it. But I was wrong. The water swept my truck off the road and down into the stream.

At least I'm not moving, I thought. And I was thankful because I could see a rescue crew coming to help me. I was worried, though. *Dad is going to be angry.*

Score	1	2	3	4

_____
_____
_____
_____
_____
_____
_____
_____
_____

Writing Rubric

Organization

	Does the writing have a clear structure and is it appropriate for the writer's audience, purpose, and type of writing	How smoothly do the ideas flow together?
4 Wow!	The writing has a structure that is <u>clear</u> and appropriate for the writer's audience, purpose, and type of writing.	The ideas progress in a smooth and orderly way. • The introduction is strong. • The **ideas** flow well from **paragraph** to **paragraph**. • The ideas in each paragraph flow well from one **sentence** to the next. • Effective **transitions** connect ideas. • The conclusion is strong.
3 Ahh.	The writing has a structure that is <u>generally</u> clear and appropriate for the writer's audience, purpose, and type of writing.	<u>Most</u> of the ideas progress in a smooth and orderly way. • The introduction is adequate. • Most of the **ideas** flow well from **paragraph** to **paragraph**. • Most ideas in each paragraph flow from one **sentence** to the next. • Effective **transitions** connect most of the ideas. • The conclusion is adequate.
2 Hmm.	The structure of the writing is <u>not</u> clear or <u>not</u> appropriate for the writer's audience, purpose, and type of writing.	<u>Some</u> of the ideas progress in a smooth and orderly way. • The introduction is weak. • Some of the **ideas** flow well from **paragraph** to **paragraph**. • Some ideas in each paragraph flow from one **sentence** to the next. • **Transitions** connect some ideas. • The conclusion is weak.
1 Huh?	The writing is not clear or organized.	<u>Few or none</u> of the ideas progress in a smooth and orderly way.

Raise the Score

1. Use the rubric on page 62 to evaluate and score this narrative.

Score	1	2	3	4

Ready

It had rained. I was home with Anna and Paul, my little sister and brother. The power went out at 6:30 p.m. The land-line phones were not working. I always make sure my cell phone is charged, so I was able to receive their calls. My parents called to tell me the roads were washed out, so they couldn't come home.

It always pays to be prepared because you just never know what might happen. I was reminded of this the other night during the big storm.

Then my other neighbor, Emil, knocked on my door. He was frantic. His pregnant wife needed to get to the hospital, but his car wouldn't start! I remembered that my dad keeps a set of jumper cables and a spare battery in the garage. I showed him where they were and he was able to start his car. (Luckily for him, the road to the hospital wasn't washed out.) At 7:15, my neighbor Sid came over and asked if I had any fuel he could use for his lantern. I loaned him one of our battery-powered lanterns. We have a few.

We had dinner—canned stew. We waited for my parents. I knew they'd be home soon because I heard on my battery-powered radio that the roads were open. We always keep canned food on hand.

When my parents arrived, they were glad that Anna, Paul, and I were safe. I was glad that my family and I always prepare for emergencies!

---

2. Explain what the writer should do to raise the score:

_____

_____

_____

3. Now revise the narrative on page 63 to improve its organization. Write your revised narrative here.

Use Transitions

Revise this narrative. Add transitions to make the paragraphs flow better.

A Lot to Be Thankful For

At 2:00 p.m. on June 24, we got in our car and left town before the hurricane hit. We moved in with my aunt that night. We've lived there ever since.

We returned a few weeks ago to see our neighborhood. The storm had done so much damage. It would have been easy to lose hope about everything. I knew I couldn't give up. There is a lot we must do before the neighborhood can be rebuilt, cleaning up trash and removing the houses that were destroyed.

Besides, there are things we can be thankful for. We're all alive and unhurt. My parents have jobs. And we have a place to stay.

And I, personally, have a lot to be thankful for. I have been studying hard in school and getting good grades. I have just won an academic scholarship. This scholarship will allow me to go to a good school, one that usually costs a lot of money to attend.

I know I'm lucky. Good luck can turn bad. I'm making the most of this chance. I plan to go to college to get a degree. I'll use that degree to build a life for myself. Then, if there is still work to be done, I'll find a way to somehow help rebuild this neighborhood.

Maybe it's foolish to have these goals. These are my goals. I have to believe I can reach them because I promised myself I wouldn't give up.

More on Transitions

Revise this narrative. Add transitions to show time and to show events or ideas in a sequence.

Lucky

I'll never forget that day. It was windy, but we had to work to protect our house from the storm. We boarded up the windows. We made sure the things outside wouldn't blow away. I called my dog, Squeaky, inside. We were ready to leave. But then we ended up staying home because we thought it would be safe enough and because Grandpa didn't want to leave.

We waited for the storm to hit. We tried to think of fun things to do. (We couldn't watch TV because the power was out.) We played card games. We told each other scary stories. They weren't very scary, though. Believe it or not, I got bored and ended up doing my homework.

When the hurricane hit, it came closer to our town than we expected. Some houses in our neighborhood were badly damaged, but luckily there was very little damage to our home.

The hurricane passed, my dad took our little boat and went to help the people in a neighborhood that was flooded. They weren't as lucky as we were.

We had been through big storms. But this hurricane was the worst storm of all time. We had not experienced anything like it.

I loved my hometown, but I don't live there. I live in a part of the country where there are no hurricanes!

© National Geographic Learning, a part of Cengage Learning, Inc.

Plan a Personal Narrative

Use pages 67–68 to plan your personal narrative.

1. What weather-related event from your life would you like to write about? List some ideas in a chart and write down the good and bad points for each idea. Circle the topic you choose.

Ideas	Good and Bad Points

2. Is your topic too broad? Use this graphic to narrow your topic.

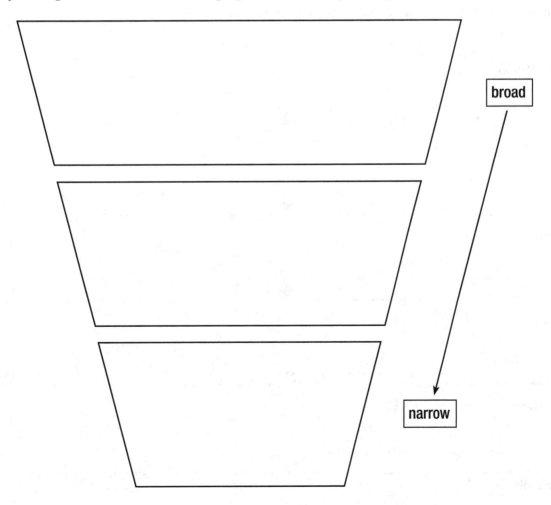

broad

narrow

3. Now gather details about the event in a five-senses diagram.

I saw . . .	
I heard . . .	
I smelled . . .	
I tasted . . .	
I touched or felt . . .	

Five-Senses Diagram

4. Use this sequence chain to plan your personal narrative.

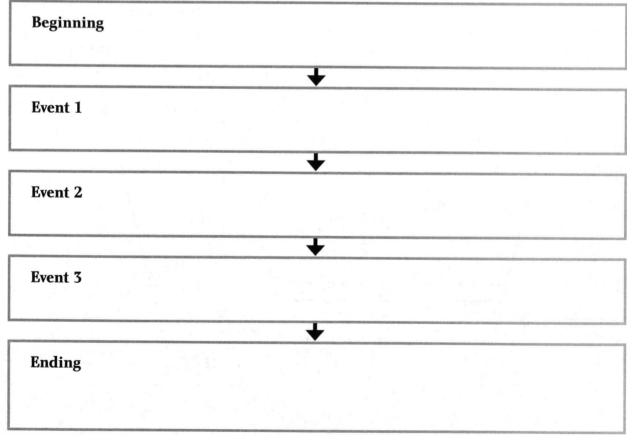

Beginning

↓

Event 1

↓

Event 2

↓

Event 3

↓

Ending

Sequence Chain

Draft a Personal Narrative

Use your plan from pages 67–68 to write the first draft of your personal narrative.

Drafting Checklist

☐ Catch the readers' interest with your introduction.

☐ Include details that let the reader "see and feel" what's happening.

☐ Tell about real events in the order they happened.

☐ Connect ideas with transitions.

☐ Express your thoughts and feelings.

☐ End by explaining what you learned, or why the event is memorable.

Draft a Personal Narrative, continued

Revise a Personal Narrative

1. Use the checklist to evaluate this draft of a personal narrative. What changes are needed?

_____

_____

_____

_____

_____

_____

Revising Checklist

☐ Are there any parts that are confusing or unclear?

☐ Do any of the parts need more detail or explanation?

☐ Are the sentences and paragraphs in the most effective order?

☐ Do the ideas flow smoothly? Do you need to add transitions?

2. Revise this draft. Use revising marks to show your changes.

Revising

MARK	WHAT IT MEANS
∧	Insert something.
↶	Move to here.
⌐	Replace with this.
⌿	Take out.
¶	Make a new paragraph.

My Earthquake Experience

I walked next door to my friend Adrian's house. I knocked on the door. The ground started to move. Pebbles hit the top of my head. In a few seconds, it was over. I didn't know why pebbles were falling. I thought it was raining pebbles!

Adrian's dad answered the door. He was in the army. "Did you feel the earthquake?" he asked. "Um...yes," I answered. I was a kid. I really didn't even know what an earthquake was. It seems funny now, but when I was a kid, it was pretty scary.

I realized what had happened. The earthquake had caused pebbles to fall from the roof onto my head.

3. Now use the checklist to help you revise the draft of your personal narrative on pages 69–70. Use a clean sheet of paper.

Edit and Proofread

Grammar Workout: Check Helping Verbs

Add a helping verb to make the meaning of each sentence more precise. You may have to change the main verb.

1. Juan knows the terrible damage an earthquake causes.

_____

2. There's no way to predict a quake but his family prepares.

_____

3. They keep extra food and water in their house.

_____

4. They need to rely on these supplies for several days.

_____

Spelling Workout: Check Suffixes

Add the suffix _–ful_ to these words.

1. beauty _____   **3.** color _____   **5.** care _____

2. mercy _____   **4.** grace _____   **6.** meaning _____

Add the suffix _–able_ to these words.

7. live _____   **9.** honor _____   **11.** misery _____

8. enjoy _____   **10.** rely _____   **12.** comfort _____

Add the suffix _–y_ to these words.

13. snow _____   **15.** mud _____   **17.** fog _____

14. juice _____   **16.** rock _____   **18.** shine _____

Edit and Proofread, continued

Mechanics Workout: Check Apostrophes in Contractions
Write contractions for the words in parentheses.

1. I was walking with Woof yesterday. _____ my dog. **(he is)**

2. He _____ wait to go for his walk each day. **(can not)**

3. We saw the Bulls at the park. _____ a softball team. **(They are)**

4. When we got home, I _____ figure out why books had fallen from my shelves. **(could not)**

5. Later I learned there had been a quake. We _____ even feel it! **(did not)**

Check Grammar, Spelling, and Mechanics
Proofread the passage. Check the spelling and the use of helping verbs and apostrophes. Correct the mistakes.

Editing and Proofreading Marks	
∧	Insert something.
∧	Add a comma.
∧	Add a semicolon.
⊙	Add a period.
⊙	Add a colon.
ᵛ ᵛ	Add quotation marks.
ᵛ	Add an apostrophe.
≡	Capitalize.
/	Make lower case.
℘	Delete.
¶	Make new paragraph.
◯	Check spelling.
⌒	Replace with this.
∽	Change order.
#	Insert space.
⌒	Close up.

Sophia and I were editing our work with red pens. I safelly say shes my best friend. Suddennly, I could'nt write straight. Our sturddy desks were shaking violentlly. I honesttly admit I was scared. Then the quake stopped. Unbelieveable!

We looked at our once beautyful papers. They had long red squiggly lines on them! I laughed. Otherwise, I have cried. "Its not funny," Sophia said angryly. "Now we have to do these over." She was miserrable.

Mr. Sato told us not to worry. He was just gratefull we werent hurt. My classmates were realy glad they did'nt have to do their papers over. I say Im completly in agreement!

Edit and Proofread Your Personal Narrative

Now edit and proofread your work.

1. Use a checklist as you edit and proofread. Add things you are working on to the checklist.

2. Look to see which errors are marked most often. Jot down your top three trouble spots.

_____

_____

_____

3. Ask your teacher about ways to fix these mistakes, or check out the Grammar Handbook for information.

Focus on Spelling

Improve your spelling by following these steps.

1. Create a personal spelling list. Record words that you misspelled. Look up the correct spelling in the dictionary and add these words to **My Spelling List**.

My Spelling List
lovable
lovely
happiness
funny
dirty

2. Pick twelve words. Focus on four words each day. Write your words before each meal and check the spelling. At the end of the week, try writing all twelve words.

3. Have a partner stand with his or her back to the board. List his or her spelling words on the board. Say each word and ask your partner to spell it. Then switch roles.

4. Organize your words into lists. List them in reverse alphabetical order. Next list them from easiest to hardest. Then list them from the shortest to longest word.

5. Invent your own acronyms. Think of a word that begins with each letter. The words in the correct order should be easy for you to remember. For example:

spelling word	acronym
ocean	**o**ctopus **c**oral **e**el **a**re **n**ear

Publish, Share, and Reflect

Publish and Share Your Personal Narrative

**Check the final formats you used to publish your personal narrative.
Then answer the following questions.**

Publishing	
What was the final format of your project?	**How did you share your project?**
☐ Wrote it neatly by hand	☐ Shared it with a large group
☐ Typed it on a computer	☐ Shared it with a small group

1. Whether you published it by hand or on the computer, what did you do to dress up your final project?

_____

_____

_____

_____

_____

2. How did you share your work? What did you learn through sharing your work?

_____

_____

_____

_____

_____

_____

_____

_____

_____

_____

_____

_____

Reflect on Your Personal Narrative

Read your personal narrative. Then answer questions 1–6.

1. What do you like best about your work? _____

_____

_____

2. What did you do well? _____

_____

_____

3. What could you improve about your work? _____

_____

_____

_____

4. What did you discover about yourself as you wrote? _____

_____

_____

5. How did your feelings about this experience change as a result of your writing

about it? _____

_____

_____

6. Will you add your personal narrative to your Writing Portfolio? Explain
your decision.

❑ Yes, I will add this to my Writing Portfolio.

_____

_____

❑ No, I will not add this to my Writing Portfolio.

_____

_____

Short Story

What makes this short story a good model? Read the story and answer the questions.

Dream Girl

by Alfonso Cruz

Don was a dork. He spent most of his time in his bedroom, doing homework. That's where he was the night he created Amanda, the girl of his dreams.

He was typing data into the "Design-a-Human" computer program he had invented. Suddenly he heard a BOOM and the lights went out. His computer started smoking. Seconds later, the lights came back on.

As the smoke cleared, there she was, standing beside Don. She was *perfect*.

Amanda slept in Don's bed that night. Don slept in a sleeping bag, on the floor.

"You're not going to wear *that*, are you?" she said the next morning. She tried to find better clothes in his closet, but gave up. "You should eat *high-fiber* cereal with *nonfat* milk," she said as he munched a bowl of Sugar Puffs.

At school, all the guys stared at her. He should've felt proud, but he still felt like a dork. "Hurry up," she said sternly as he fumbled for his books. Amanda turned to walk down the hall. Don rushed to follow her, and he stumbled and fell. "You are such a DORK," Amanda said, and everyone laughed, including her.

BEEP! BEEP! BEEP! Don's alarm clock awakened him. He had fallen asleep in front of his computer. Don looked around. He was alone in his room. That's when he knew that Amanda had just been a dream—and he smiled.

Feature Checklist

A good short story

- ☐ provides background about the setting
- ☐ has a plot that makes sense and keeps readers' interest
- ☐ has one or more characters
- ☐ usually has dialogue between characters.

1. Circle the characters in the story.

2. Underline the words that show the setting.

3. Number the key events in the plot in order.

4. What does the dialogue—or lack of dialogue—reveal about each character?

   _____
   _____
   _____
   _____
   _____
   _____
   _____
   _____
   _____

5. What is the conflict, or problem, in this story?

   _____
   _____
   _____
   _____
   _____
   _____
   _____

Focus on Character

Read the following character description. Then improve the description using each technique below.

> Reggie wasn't your typical teenager. He had a secret. But it only revealed itself once a month. On nights with a full moon, Reggie became a werewolf!

1. Descriptive Details

_____

_____

_____

_____

_____

2. Character's Actions

_____

_____

_____

_____

_____

3. Character's Words and Thoughts

_____

_____

_____

_____

_____

4. Reactions of Other Characters

_____

_____

_____

_____

_____

Focus on Setting

Choose one of the setting options below. Think about the details of the setting. Write your ideas in the graphic organizer.

Time	
Place	
Sights	
Sounds	
Feelings	
How it affects the characters	
How it affects the action	

Using your graphic organizer, write the first few lines of a story. Remember to grab the readers' interest right away and use a lot of sensory details to describe the setting.

_____

_____

_____

_____

_____

_____

Focus on Plot

Read the following short story. Then fill out the plot diagram on page 81.

The New Kid

When Anya heard they were going to have a new student in their class, she was excited. She had been the new kid for the past two months. She was still too shy to make friends. Maybe she would get along with this new kid.

The next day, the new student arrived and the teacher introduced him. "Everyone," she said. "This is Manik. He's from India, and he doesn't speak much English yet, so please make him feel welcome."

From India! Anya thought, pleased. Her own family was from India. She had been born in the United States and only knew English, but her parents spoke Hindi. Maybe they would be able to talk to Manik and help him learn English.

At lunch, she approached Manik sitting by himself. He looked at her, and all at once she remembered that they didn't speak the same language. She hesitated, embarrassed, then said, "Hindi?"

His face lit up in a smile. "Yes," he said, nodding eagerly.

"My house after school?" Anya asked. Manik nodded. He could understand her, even if he couldn't answer her.

When Anya took Manik to her house, her parents were delighted to meet him. They invited him to stay for dinner, and the four of them talked in English and Hindi, helping Manik learn. They were so happy that Anya had finally made a friend.

Focus on Plot, continued

Fill out the plot diagram below.

The New Kid

Characters: _____
_____
_____

Setting: _____
_____
_____

Turning Point

Solution

Problem

Focus on Point of View

Rewrite the story on page 80. Use the first-person point of view.

_____

_____

_____

_____

_____

_____

_____

_____

_____

_____

_____

_____

_____

_____

_____

_____

_____

_____

_____

_____

_____

_____

_____

_____

_____

_____

_____

_____

_____

_____

_____

_____

_____

_____

_____

Level A
Project 8: Write as a Storyteller
82
Model Study: Focus on Point of View

Evaluate for Voice and Style

Read each story. Use the rubric on page 84 to score each story for voice and style. Explain your scores.

Writing Sample 1

A Scary Time

Alice challenged Sarun to knock on the shack's door. The shack was abandoned. Most kids were afraid to go near it. But not Sarun.

Alice and Sarun waited until dark. A couple of friends came by, too. Sarun opened the gate.

Sarun was thinking about ghosts when he saw something move. That startled him a little. He was a little afraid then. But, he went up to the door anyway.

Sarun got to the door and raised his hand to knock. Then he heard a loud noise. The loud bang was from inside. He saw a cat jump out. Everyone screamed. But Sarun just laughed.

Score	1	2	3	4

Writing Sample 2

The Haunted Shack

Alice dared Sarun to knock on the abandoned shack's door. Most kids stayed far away. But Sarun rarely backed down from a challenge.

The two of them waited until dark. A couple of friends came by to witness Sarun's bravery. Very courageously he slowly opened the gate. "It's not too late to change your mind," said Alice.

Determined, Sarun marched up to the front door. "There are no ghosts," he thought. But just then he saw something move. A cold chill streaked down his back.

Finally, Sarun reached the door. As he raised his hand to knock, a loud bang rang out from inside. Before he had a chance to react, a stray cat leapt out from a broken window! His friends screamed. But Sarun had the last laugh!

Score	1	2	3	4

Writing Rubric

Voice and Style

	Does the writing have a clear voice and is it the best style for the type of writing?	Is the language interesting and are the words and sentences appropriate for the purpose, audience, and type of writing?
4 Wow!	The writing <u>fully</u> engages the reader with its individual voice. The writing style is best for the type of writing.	The words and sentences are interesting and appropriate to the purpose and audience. · The words are precise and engaging. · The sentences are varied and flow together smoothly.
3 Ahh.	<u>Most</u> of the writing engages the reader with an individual voice. The writing style is mostly best for the type of writing.	<u>Most</u> of the words and sentences are interesting and appropriate to the purpose and audience. · Most words are precise and engaging. · Most sentences are varied and flow together.
2 Hmm.	<u>Some</u> of the writing engages the reader, but it has no individual voice and the style is not best for the writing type.	<u>Some</u> of the words and sentences are interesting and appropriate to the purpose and audience. · Some words are precise and engaging. · Some sentences are varied, but the flow could be smoother.
1 Huh?	The writing does <u>not</u> engage the reader.	<u>Few or none</u> of the words and sentences are appropriate to the purpose and audience. · The words are often vague and dull. · The sentences lack variety and do not flow together.

Raise the Score

1. Use the rubric on page 84 to evaluate and score this story.

Score	1	2	3	4

Abandoned

One day, Mira was sitting on her porch. All her friends had gone to camp. But her family couldn't afford it.

It was getting stormy, so Mira went inside. As she got up, she heard something. When she looked, she saw a tiny kitten in the bushes.

The cat was very thin and dirty. It was starting to rain. Mira didn't want to leave this abandoned kitten in the rain. She picked him up and carried him inside.

Her mother saw her right away. She said she couldn't keep him. But Mira didn't want to keep him. She just wanted to foster him until they could find a home for him.

Her mother agreed. The next day they posted signs everywhere. It wasn't long before a young woman called. She was interested in the cat.

Mira felt sad that she couldn't keep the cat herself. But, at the same time, she was happy that he now had a good home.

---

2. Explain what the writer should do to raise the score.

_____

_____

_____

3. **Now revise the story on page 85 to improve its voice and style. Write your
   revised story here.**

_____

_____

_____

_____

_____

_____

_____

_____

_____

_____

_____

_____

_____

_____

_____

_____

_____

_____

_____

_____

_____

_____

Use Effective Words

Edit the paragraphs. Replace the underlined words with specific or more descriptive words from the chart.

NOUNS	VERBS	ADJECTIVES	ADVERBS
nightmares	reassured	frightening	gently
comedy	determined	humorous	soothingly
multiplex	attempted	hectic	nervously
films	prevent	jammed	fearfully

Dragged and Grabbed

Matthew wasn't a fan of <u>scary</u> movies. That didn't <u>stop</u> his friends from dragging him to a monster movie at the local theater. It was a <u>busy</u> Saturday afternoon. The theater was <u>crowded</u>.

"Are you sure these <u>movies</u> won't give me <u>bad dreams</u>?" asked Matthew <u>uneasily</u>. "No," his friends <u>told</u> him. At the last moment, Matthew <u>decided</u> he couldn't do it. He <u>tried</u> to turn back, but his friends grabbed him <u>softly</u> by the arm and said, "Wait! Why don't we watch a <u>funny movie</u> instead?"

Edit the paragraphs. Replace dull or vague words with specific and more colorful words. Add similes and metaphors, too.

Matthew's fear of scary movies started when he was younger. His parents unknowingly let him watch a movie about bad clowns. The skin on the clowns' faces drooped down. Their mouths were bright red semicircles starting at the top of one cheek and curving around up to the other. Their eyes were large and round.

Matthew was afraid of what he saw. He couldn't sleep that night. He was afraid the clowns would come into his room. Those images have been with him ever since.

But Matthew's friends love movies about creatures. They prefer to watch them on a big screen. Some of their favorites are the classic ones. Matthew's best friend Brian even dresses up like the Wolf Man every Halloween.

Vary Your Sentences

Edit the passage for sentence variety. Use different sentence beginnings and different sentence types.

Try Something Exciting!

Thrill seekers are people who enjoy adventure and fast-paced action. Thrill seekers enjoy activities that other people might be too scared to try. Thrill seekers might try bungee jumping or hang gliding.

Dante and Malik are thrill seekers. They are good friends and both enjoy the thrill of being scared. They are always ready for the rides at the amusement park. They try to go whenever they can.

The boys especially love roller coasters. The boys discovered a new one at Funscape Park. The boys waited for hours to ride the Flying Demon on Saturday. The wait was worth it. The roller coaster was amazingly fast and had intense twists and loops. The ride was thrilling.

Edit the passage. Make some sentences long and some short.

Famous Monsters

Vampires are some of the most famous monsters in all of fiction. Vampires can be found in stories from Africa to Asia. The vampire's popularity can be traced back to as early the eighteenth and nineteenth centuries. Bram Stoker's *Dracula* was published in 1897. It was published over 200 years ago. It is still considered the most influential vampire story.

The story of Count Dracula has inspired many different movies. One of the earliest films was the silent movie *Nosferatu*. It was made in Germany. The year was 1921. It starred the actor Max Schreck. Ten years later, Universal Studios released its own Dracula. The movie *Dracula* starred Bela Lugosi. Later interpretations of Dracula featured different actors. Christopher Lee, Frank Langella, and Gary Oldman have played the Count. Universal's original Dracula is the image most people associate with the character.

© National Geographic Learning, a part of Cengage Learning, Inc.

Combine Sentences

Edit the passage. Use connecting words (*and, but, or, while, when, as, before, after*) to join sentences that are next to each other or have repeated or related ideas.

Searching for Vampires

The cavern was dark. Bruce couldn't see anything. He thought he heard bat wings flapping in the distance. He was not frightened. "It's no big deal," said Bruce. "It's not like there are really vampires down here."

He got near the end of the tunnel. He saw a light flicker behind him. "What was that?" he thought to himself. He turned around. He saw his brother Chris following him with a flashlight.

"You shouldn't be down here," said Chris. "You know there are vampires in these caves." Chris stood still. Bruce kept walking into the darkness. He vanished out of Chris's sight. Bruce turned toward his brother. He said, "I'll prove to the whole town that vampires don't exist!"

"You have two options, Bruce," said Chris. "You can turn around and save yourself. You can keep going and never be heard from again." Chris finished his warning. He heard Bruce scream loudly, like a little girl. Suddenly, Bruce was running toward the entrance of the cave at full speed.

Bruce sprinted past Chris out of the cave. Chris tried to run after him. He was so scared that he nearly fell. When Chris finally got outside, Bruce was bent over, laughing. "Gotcha!" he said to Chris.

Combine Sentences, continued

Combine sentences by moving details from one sentence into another.

1.

Bruce bravely headed into the cave. He was determined to prove vampires were not real.	_____ _____ _____ _____

2.

He was nervous as he approached the cave entrance. He could hear faint noises coming from inside the cave.	_____ _____ _____ _____

Combine sentences by using fewer words to say the same thing.

3.

Bruce couldn't see inside the cave, it was just too dark. But he knew in his heart and soul that he had to prove his bravery to everyone. He especially wanted to prove it to Jillian.	_____ _____ _____ _____ _____ _____ _____

4.

Chris was worried about his older brother's stubbornness. He had tried for days and weeks to stop Bruce from even thinking about going into the cave. Bruce wouldn't stop to listen to Chris's reasons.	_____ _____ _____ _____ _____ _____ _____

Plan Your Own Version of a Story

Use pages 93–94 to plan your own version of a story.

1. Decide What to Change

Create a chart to compare the original story with your new version.

	Original Story	My Story
Characters		
Setting		
Plot		
Point of View		

2. Plan Your Characters

Use a web to name and describe each character in your version of the story.

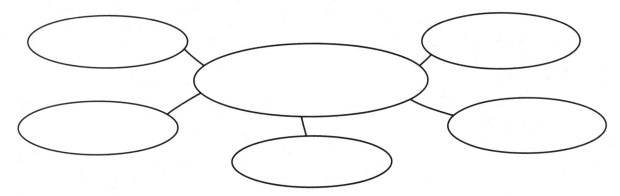

3. Plan Your Setting

Fill out a web with details about where and when your version of the story takes place.

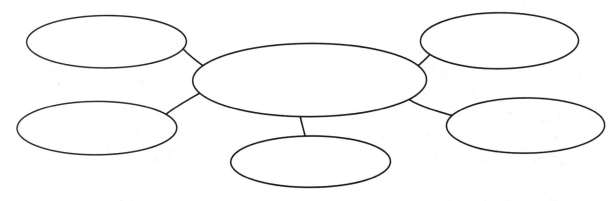

4. Plan Your Plot

What will happen in your story? Use a plot diagram to plan the action.

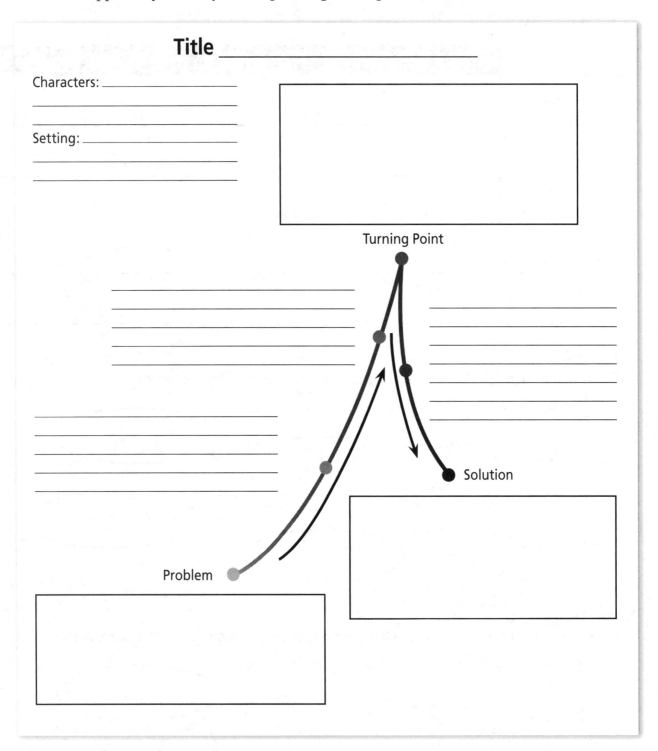

5. Choose a Point of View

Will you write the story in first person or third person? Try a few different points of view and decide which is the most interesting. Remember, a narrator can only tell what he or she knows.

Draft a Story

Use your plan from pages 93–94 to write the first draft of your story.

Drafting Checklist

- ☐ Introduce your characters and the setting in the beginning.
- ☐ Develop a plot that centers on a problem a character has to solve.
- ☐ Use plenty of details and colorful language to make your characters and setting come alive.
- ☐ Vary your sentences to keep your readers engaged.

_____

_____

_____

_____

_____

_____

_____

_____

_____

_____

_____

_____

_____

_____

_____

_____

_____

_____

_____

_____

_____

_____

_____

_____

Draft a Story, continued

Revise a Story

1. Use the checklist to evaluate this draft of a story. What changes are needed?

_____

_____

_____

_____

_____

© National Geographic Learning, a part of Cengage Learning, Inc.

Revising Checklist

☐ Are the sentences varied? Are some sentences short and some long? Are there different kinds?

☐ Are there sentences that can be combined?

☐ Is the writing engaging and interesting? Do you need to replace any words with more powerful or descriptive words?

2. Revise this draft. Use revising marks to show your changes.

Revising

MARK	WHAT IT MEANS
∧	Insert something.
↶	Move to here.
⌐	Replace with this.
˗	Take out.
¶	Make a new paragraph.

Alien America

Xio's first day of work was hard. It was a hot day. He was starting work in the produce department at the grocery store. On the way, his UFO broke down. Xio ran to work, but he was late.

Xio's new boss yelled at him for being late. His co-workers made fun of the way he looked. Xio was so upset. He couldn't focus. He kept dropping things all day. Lunchtime came. Xio realized that he forgot to bring money. By the time his shift was over he was hungry.

On his way home, Xio's boss stopped him. Xio was happy. He told Xio that he did well for his first day.

3. Now use the checklist to help you revise the draft of your story on pages 95–96. Use a clean sheet of paper.

Edit and Proofread

Grammar Workout: Check for Adjectives and Adverbs

Add adjectives and adverbs to add color and richness to the sentences.

1. The robot strutted down the hallway.

_____

2. Its feet clanked on the floor.

_____

3. Miss Petal's cat found a place to hide.

_____

4. People on the street were afraid of the robot.

_____

5. Ms. Rosario watched the news for warnings about the robot.

_____

Spelling Workout: Check Adverbs Ending in –ly

Add –ly to these adjectives to form adverbs.

1. sneaky _____   **7.** tense _____   **13.** attractive _____

2. ideal _____   **8.** cruel _____   **14.** rude _____

3. angry _____   **9.** polite _____   **15.** willful _____

4. crazy _____   **10.** cheerful _____   **16.** wise _____

5. delightful _____   **11.** eerie _____   **17.** nasty _____

6. immediate _____   **12.** pretty _____   **18.** bashful _____

Edit and Proofread, continued

Mechanics Workout: Check Punctuation in Dialogue

Proofread the following sentences for correct punctuation.

1. Miss Petal screamed at the robot "Get out of here!

2. I'm calling the police," I said.

3. "Don't call the police. They'll take him away whispered Dr. Frankenstein.

4. The robot looked at Miss Petal and asked, Do you have food"

5. Is this enough? she asked as she handed him a turkey.

Check Grammar, Spelling, and Mechanics

**Proofread the passage. Check the spelling and punctuation in the dialogue.
Find opportunities to add adjectives and adverbs.**

Editing and Proofreading Marks	
∧	Insert something.
⩑	Add a comma.
⩘	Add a semicolon.
⊙	Add a period.
⊙	Add a colon.
⌄⌄	Add quotation marks.
⌄	Add an apostrophe.
≡	Capitalize.
/	Make lower case.
⟍	Delete.
¶	Make new paragraph.
◯	Check spelling.
⌒	Replace with this.
∼	Change order.
#	Insert space.
⌒	Close up.

The robot was eerilly calm, but Miss Petal knew it wanted food. So she ran into the kitchen to get food. She came back with her arms full. She had apples, potatoes, and a whole chicken. She threw the food on the table and ran to hide. She watched the robot immediatly eat the food.

More food the robot said.

Miss Petal ran back into the kitchen and brought out even more food. She had loaves of bread, cheese, a whole ham, and a pie. The robot cheerfuly kept eating.

More food! the robot demanded.

"I don't have any more food" Miss Petal said.

Edit and Proofread Your Story

Now edit and proofread your work.

1. Use the checklist as you edit and proofread. Add things you are working on to the checklist.

2. Look to see which errors are marked most often. Jot down your top three trouble spots.

_____

_____

_____

3. Ask your teacher about ways to fix these mistakes, or check out the Grammar Handbook for information.

Focus on Spelling

Improve your spelling by following these steps.

1. Create a personal spelling list. Record words that you misspelled. Look up the correct spelling in the dictionary and add these words to **My Spelling List**.

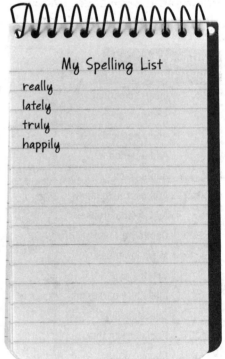

My Spelling List
really
lately
truly
happily

2. Pick twelve words. Make a colorful display of the words. Get a sheet of chart paper. Write each word three times in a different color.

3. Work with a partner to play **Spelling Tic-Tac-Toe**. Draw a tic-tac-toe board. Take turns asking each other to spell words. When a player spells a word correctly, that player gets to mark an X or an O on the game board.

4. Write the letters for each word on separate squares of paper. Attach the letters for each word to each other with a paper clip. Unscramble the letters to spell each of your words.

5. Invent your own memory strategy for difficult words. Think of a good way to remember *why* letters appear or not in a word. For example:

Word: dessert
Explanation: "It has two s's for <u>s</u>weet <u>s</u>tuff!"

Publish, Share, and Reflect

Publish and Share Your Story

**Check the final formats you used to publish your story.
Then answer the following questions.**

Publishing	
What was the final format of your project?	**How did you share your project?**
☐ Wrote it neatly by hand	☐ Shared it with a large group
☐ Typed it on a computer	☐ Shared it with a small group

1. Whether you published it by hand or on the computer, what did you do to dress up your final project?

_____

_____

_____

_____

_____

2. How did you share your work? What did you learn through sharing your work?

_____

_____

_____

_____

_____

_____

_____

_____

_____

_____

_____

_____

_____

Reflect on Your Story

Read your story. Then answer questions 1–6.

1. What do you like best about your work? _____

_____

_____

2. What did you do well? _____

_____

_____

3. What could you improve about your work? _____

_____

_____

4. What was fun about rewriting a story? Are there other stories you could rewrite? _____

_____

_____

5. How did you put your own personal stamp on the story? _____

_____

_____

6. Will you add your story to your Writing Portfolio? Explain your decision.

❏ Yes, I will add this to my Writing Portfolio.

_____

_____

❏ No, I will not add this to my Writing Portfolio.

_____

_____

Information Report

What makes this report a good model? Read it and answer the questions.

Searching for Water in Outer Space

by Chris Gonzales

Is there life on other planets? To answer this question, scientists look for one important clue: water. Life cannot exist without water. Scientists look for water on other planets. They use advanced tools to do this. One of these tools is the Hubble Telescope. It helps scientists learn about places in outer space where there might be water. Where there is water, there might be life.

Used to observe distant planets, the Hubble was launched into space in 1990 (Pearson 24). It travels about 375 miles above Earth. There, it can peer deep into space (Pearson 25). The Hubble takes pictures that help us learn about remote parts of the universe.

In 2007, Hubble took pictures of a planet called HD 209458b. It is 150 light years from Earth (Gardner 14). Imagine a space shuttle traveling 18,000 miles per hour. It would take almost 3 million years to reach HD 209458b (Gardner 16)! The Hubble didn't have to travel to the planet. It took pictures from far away.

The Hubble pictures showed that HD 209458b contains water vapor (Pearson 32). Water vapor is water in the form of gas. If it is present in the atmosphere, then water might exist on the planet itself (Pearson 33).

Feature Checklist

A good information report

- [ ] tells about a topic in an interesting way
- [ ] has an introduction, body, and conclusion
- [ ] has a clear central idea
- [ ] uses facts and details to support the central idea.

1. **How does the writer make the topic interesting?**

    _____

    _____

    _____

    _____

2. **How does the beginning get the readers' attention?**

    _____

    _____

    _____

    _____

3. **What is the central idea of the report?**

    _____

    _____

    _____

    _____

4. **List one main idea of the report and the details that support it.**

    _____

    _____

    _____

    _____

    _____

    _____

Finding water on another planet may not seem important. After all, water can be found everywhere on Earth. But life on Earth could not exist without water. Living creatures need water to survive (Ellis 45). Water vapor exists in the atmosphere of HD 209458b. Does that mean life existed there at some time? Perhaps!

Scientists have used the Hubble in the search for life on Mars. In 2007, the Hubble allowed scientists to observe the surface of Mars closely (Pearson 26). They found something interesting. Mars may have once had water beneath its surface (Pearson 27).

If so, water seeped above ground. It was exposed to higher temperatures. Then it turned into gas. Mars was left with a rocky surface (Gardner 30). If there is still water under the surface, life may exist there. One day, we might know for sure.

The Hubble reveals new discoveries about the universe. As technology advances, scientists can search for other signs of life.

The universe is still a great mystery. Technology allows us to learn more about whatever—and whoever—is out there.

5. List another main idea and the details that support it.

_____

_____

_____

_____

_____

_____

6. How does the conclusion reinforce the central idea?

_____

_____

_____

_____

Evaluate for Focus and Unity

Read these paragraphs from an information report. Use the rubric on page 106 to score each report for focus and unity. Explain your scores.

Writing Sample 1

Why Pluto Isn't a Planet

Our solar system used to have nine planets. But in 2006, scientists changed their minds. They decided that the smallest planet wasn't really a planet after all. Pluto is no longer considered a planet. How did scientists make this decision?

Pluto was discovered in 1930 (DeBlase 56). Soon, asteroids, moons, and other objects were discovered. Some were bigger than Pluto (DeBlase 58). Yet they were not considered planets. No one had a clear definition of what a planet was. So people could not explain why these objects were not called planets. In 2006, scientists decided that since Pluto was not large enough to pull objects into its orbit, it was not a planet.

Score	1	2	3	4

_____
_____
_____
_____
_____
_____
_____

Writing Sample 2

Is Pluto a Planet?

Astronomers now agree on criteria for a planet. A heavenly body must be large enough to pull other objects into its orbit. Otherwise, it is not a planet. Pluto is very small. So its own orbit wobbles when it nears Neptune (Durham 19). Pluto was named after the Roman god of the underworld (Bostock 10). Pluto has little effect on the objects around it. It affects only its moon. Pluto's moon is Charon. Earth also has a moon. But it is not named.

Not everyone agrees that Pluto isn't really a planet. Some people think any round object that isn't a star should be considered a planet. That would increase the number of known planets to 50 (Hatch 49). Our solar system would be filled with planets! Our sun is actually a star. But it's big enough to be a planet.

Score	1	2	3	4

_____
_____
_____
_____
_____
_____
_____
_____

Writing Rubric

Focus and Unity

	How clearly does the writing present a central idea or claim?	How well does everything go together?
4 Wow!	The writing expresses a <u>clear</u> central idea or claim about the topic.	<u>Everything</u> in the writing goes together. · The main idea of each paragraph goes with the central idea or claim of the paper. · The main idea and details within each paragraph are related. · The conclusion is about the central idea or claim.
3 Ahh.	The writing expresses a <u>generally</u> clear central idea or claim about the topic.	<u>Most</u> parts of the writing go together. · The main idea of most paragraphs goes with the central idea or claim of the paper. · In most paragraphs, the main idea and details are related. · Most of the conclusion is about the central idea or claim.
2 Hmm.	The writing includes a topic, but the central idea or claim is <u>not</u> clear.	<u>Some</u> parts of the writing go together. · The main idea of some paragraphs goes with the central idea or claim of the paper. · In some paragraphs, the main idea and details are related. · Some of the conclusion is about the central idea or claim.
1 Huh?	The writing includes many topics and <u>does not</u> express one central idea or claim.	The parts of the writing <u>do not</u> go together. · Few paragraphs have a main idea, or the main idea does not go with the central idea or claim of the paper. · Few paragraphs contain a main idea and related details. · None of the conclusion is about the central idea or claim.

Raise the Score

1. Use the rubric on page 106 to evaluate and score this information report.

Score	1	2	3	4

Parallax: Two Eyes Are Better Than One

People have wondered about the stars for centuries. How far away are they? Scientists have developed ways of figuring out the distances of many stars.

In 1838, a German scientist discovered a way to measure the distance of stars from Earth (Aranda 32). His name was Friedrich Bessel. His discovery changed the way scientists measure stars. The discovery is called parallax (34).

People use parallax every day. When you catch a baseball, you are using parallax. My dad and I go to baseball games a lot. I'm not very good at baseball. But with practice I will get better.

Parallax depends on having two points from which to look at and measure an object (Thompson 21). For example, think about holding a pencil an arm's length from your face. Keep the pencil still. If you close one eye, then the other, the pencil seems to jump back and forth. You use both eyes to see where it actually is. This is parallax.

Bessel thought parallax might work for learning about stars. He measured the distance of a nearby star. He figured out that it was about 10 light-years away from Earth (Aranda 40). That sounds like a long way. But it is actually close to Earth compared with most other stars (41).

Scientists still use parallax to learn about stars. They do this by looking at the stars from more than one position (Collins 13). They can use two huge telescopes placed on either side of the Earth to observe the stars (Collins 16). My uncle has a telescope, too. Sometimes, we use it to look at the stars.

Other scientists have developed a satellite that they've launched into space. This satellite can determine parallax for many more stars (Collins 19). Now scientists can map the locations of millions of stars (Collins 20).

Scientists have made a lot of amazing discoveries. I'm very interested in discoveries about space. Scientists are constantly discovering things on Earth, too. Maybe I will become a scientist when I grow up.

2. Explain what the writer should do to raise the score.

_____

_____

_____

3. Now revise the information report on page 107 to improve its focus and unity. Write your revised report here.

Plan Your Research

Use this page and the next to plan your research.

1. List some topics that interest you. Choose one and circle it. Then, ask yourself
what you want to know and list research questions for the topic.

Topic for Discovery	Research Questions

2. Use this diagram to focus your topic and make it specific. Make the topic more
specific and focused at each step in the diagram.

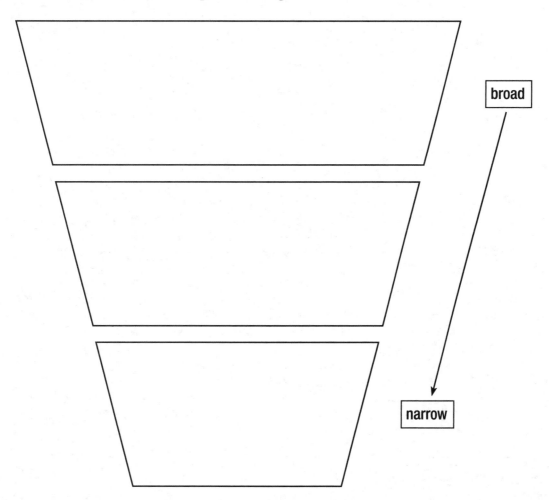

broad

narrow

3. Break down your main research question into more specific questions. Write them on the cards.

Research Questions

Locate Sources of Information

Write down some ideas for the kinds of sources you could use to find information for your information report.

_____

_____

_____

_____

_____

_____

_____

_____

_____

_____

Now, list five interview questions you would ask an expert on your topic.

1. _____

_____

_____

2. _____

_____

_____

3. _____

_____

_____

4. _____

_____

_____

5. _____

_____

_____

Look at the words in each box. Then write the words in alphabetical order.

WORD LIST	
Hubble	fossil
planet	water
star	

1. _fossil_
2. _____
3. _____
4. _____
5. _____

WORD LIST	
atmosphere	Apollo
alien	astronomer
air	

11. _____
12. _____
13. _____
14. _____
15. _____

WORD LIST	
moon	meteorite
Martian	mission
maps	

6. _____
7. _____
8. _____
9. _____
10. _____

WORD LIST	
caps	chemicals
clouds	canals
canyons	

16. _____
17. _____
18. _____
19. _____
20. _____

Evaluate Sources

Look at these print sources. Then answer the questions.

One famous comet was "discovered" by Edmond Halley. In 1705, Halley made a prediction. He said that a comet last observed in 1682 would return in 1758. In late 1758, Halley was proven correct. The comet was observed in the night sky. This observation supported Halley's belief that the comet orbited the Sun. Halley became famous for his work. The comet he observed was named after him. It's now called Halley's Comet.

—BY SUSAN REYES

from *Space Discoveries*, 2007

Dr. Reyes teaches astronomy at Middletown College.

On my camping trip last summer, I saw an amazing sight. It was a dark night. My friends and I were stargazing. Then, out of nowhere, something flew across the sky! It looked smaller than a penny. It was bright white, and it moved very quickly. It might have made a noise, too. I think we saw Halley's Comet!

—BY ALEX PETERSEN

from *True Space Stories for Kids*, 1999

Alex Petersen is a senior at Freemont High School.

1. Who wrote the material that appears in each print source?

_____

_____

2. What is the purpose of each print source? Explain your answer.

_____

_____

3. Which source is more likely to be accurate and reliable? Explain your answer.

_____

_____

_____

Look at the Web site. Then answer the questions.

http://www.mystarblog.com

MYSTARBLOG.COM

September 2006

Stargazing is great! My interest began, when I was little. Last year for my 12th brithday, my grandmother gave me a telescope. Since then, I spend every night looking at stars. Did you know the Sun is a star too. I wonder if anyone in space ever looks up at it.

This Web site is all about stars. You'll find star charts, maps, pictures, and more! Plus you can read about my own ideas. I'll tell you why the Sun is the hottest star. I'll also explain how humans can live their someday.

CLICK HERE to view a list of some cool movie's and books about stars!

1. Did the writer put a lot of time and care into the Web site? How can you tell?

_____

_____

2. When did the writer last update the site?

_____

_____

3. What kind of site is this? Explain your answer.

_____

_____

4. How could you check to see if the facts on this page are true?

_____

_____

5. Would you use this site as a source for a report on stars? Why or why not?

_____

_____

Locate Relevant Information

Skim and scan this magazine article. Then answer the questions.

NASA Discovers Avalanche on Mars

Avalanches are not unusual events on Earth. It's not too surprising when a mass of snow or rocks slides down a mountain slope. But what if that mountain is on another planet? For the first time, scientists have observed an avalanche on Mars.

How the Discovery Was Made

The space agency NASA has sent many spacecraft to Mars. One type of spacecraft is called an orbiter. It circles Mars and takes pictures. A NASA orbiter took a photograph of the avalanche on Mars. Then, it sent the picture back to NASA. Scientists were surprised to see the image.

Learning More

Finding out that there are avalanches on Mars was an exciting discovery. Now, though, scientists have a new job. They will try to find out as much as they can about the avalanches. What causes them? What are they made of? When do they happen? Answering these questions will help us learn more about Mars.

1. What do the title and beginning sentences tell you about the article's topic?

_____

_____

2. What do the keywords and headings tell you about the second paragraph of the article?

_____

_____

3. Would this article be useful to someone writing about the exploration of Mars? Why or why not?

_____

_____

_____

Skim and scan this table of contents and index from the same book. Then, answer the questions.

Contents

Index

1. Which chapter might tell how a dwarf planet differs from other planets? _____

2. Do you think you could use this book to learn about Halley's Comet? Why or why not? _____

_____

3. On what page might you find information about the rings of Saturn? _____

4. What information about the Sun could you most likely find in this book? _____

_____

_____

5. Would this book be useful if you were writing about the solar system? Why or why not?

_____

Now, skim and scan the sources you listed on page 111. Which ones should you read more carefully?

How to Take Notes

Read the excerpt from the article. Then, answer the questions.

The Great Red Spot   1
By Eva Liu

   The Great Red Spot is a giant red oval on the planet Jupiter. It is one of the planet's most noticeable features. It is also one of the strangest.

   The spot was discovered in 1664 by Robert Hooke, an English scientist. Hooke used a telescope to observe the Great Red Spot. Ever since its discovery, people have asked questions about it. Scientists have used spacecraft to study it. In 1979, a spacecraft sent pictures of the spot back to Earth. More recently, other spacecraft have explored the spot. Still, the spot remains mysterious.

   The Great Red Spot is more than a red dot. It's actually a huge storm. This storm has lasted for at least 300 years. Inside the Great Red Spot, wind can reach speeds of 250 miles per hour. The spot is thousands of miles wide. It's bigger than Earth and Mars put together.

1. Why should you take notes when you read or research a topic?

_____

2. What should you do to show that you copied the exact words from a source?

_____

3. Why should you write down the author and page number of a source?

_____

4. After reading this article, what information would you record about the author's name and the page number?

_____

5. What is one important fact from the article?

_____

See how a student used note cards to take notes on the excerpt from the article on page 117.

How have scientists examined the Great Red Spot?	What are the features of the Great Red Spot?
— Robert Hooke used a telescope to find it	— over 300 years old
— scientists have sent spacecraft to look at it	— winds of 250 miles per hour
— spacecraft sent back photos of the spot	— thousands of miles wide
Liu, page 1	Liu, page 1

Now, make your own note cards. Use them to take notes on the sources you have decided to use for your report.

How to Take Notes, continued

Practice Paraphrasing

Read the sources. Then, put the important ideas in your own words.

Scientists Find that Rings Are Recycled

By Dr. Orrin Cody

Scientists have learned more about the rings that surround some planets, such as Saturn. They have found that the rings form from dust and other materials from nearby moons. When these moons get hit by comets or asteroids, pieces of the moons fly off into the air. These pieces join to form rings around Jupiter, Saturn, Uranus, and Neptune.

38

Scientists Find Fifth Planet in Outside System

By Louis Randstad

Scientists believe they have found the largest system of planets outside of our own. It is located in the constellation Cancer. So far astronomers have discovered five planets there.

The fifth planet in this system was discovered in 2007, and scientists believe there are many more in orbit. The area around this planet is said to be fairly warm, much like Earth. However, unlike Earth, the planet is very large and made of various gases. It probably cannot support life.

At a Glance

To paraphrase:

- Read the source carefully.
- Think about the main ideas and details.
- Record important information in your own words.
- Keep your paraphrase the same length as the original.

1. What have scientists learned about rings around planets?

2. What do we know about the constellation Cancer?

Using Direct Quotes

On each index card, record an important quote from the article. Use ellipses or brackets as needed.

Follow these tips when you use a direct quote:

- copy the words exactly
- use quotation marks around any words you copy exactly from the source.

Milky Way Mystery

by Erik Polis

Scientists have made a new discovery about our Milky Way. It might be much bigger than they thought. The Milky Way has two companions in space. They are called the Large and Small Magellanic Clouds. These clouds are miniature galaxies. They have a gravitational link to our own galaxy.

A recent study revealed something about the Clouds. They are moving very fast. They're dashing through space nearly twice as fast as we thought!

This raises some new ideas about the Milky Way. One idea is that the Milky Way is twice as vast as we thought. That's the only way it could hold its grip on the speedy Magellanic Clouds. Another idea is that the Clouds are not really bound to the Milky Way. Either way, we know that our Milky Way Galaxy still holds some surprises. New discoveries await us.

87

Magellanic Clouds

Magellanic Clouds

Magellanic Clouds

Now, make note cards for information from your sources. Use what you have learned about what to put on a note card, how to paraphrase, and how to use direct quotes.

How to Decide on a Central Idea

Read each set of note cards. Then write a research question and a central idea for each set.

Set 1

How is Jupiter like a star and like a planet?
—made of materials that are also found in stars
—like a star, it generates some heat

Eady, page 42

How is Jupiter like a star and like a planet?
—if Jupiter had a lot more mass, it could become a star
—scientists call it a "failed star"

Gray, page 84

How is Jupiter like a star and like a planet?
—like a star, it is made of gas and has a core
—Jupiter's core is made of rock, like the cores of other planets

Eady, page 49

How is Jupiter like a star and like a planet?
—like other planets, it has moons that orbit it
—orbits the Sun like other planets in our solar system do

Alexander, page 75

Research Question

_____
_____
_____
_____

Central Idea

_____
_____
_____
_____

Level A
Project 9: Write as a Researcher
121
Research Strategy: How to Decide on a Central Idea

Set 2

Why isn't Pluto a planet?
—it is similar to objects near it that aren't
  planets
—it hasn't cleared the area around its orbit
  like other planets have

                          Lassiter, page 112

Why isn't Pluto a planet?
—it is much smaller than any of the other
  planets
—it is even smaller than some moons in the
  solar system

                          Armstrong, page 35

Why isn't Pluto a planet?
—it doesn't orbit the Sun in a circle like the
  other planets
—classified as a dwarf planet

                          Kwon, page 98

Why isn't Pluto a planet?
—when it was first called a planet, people
  thought it was much bigger
—some astronomers think it should never have
  been called a planet

                          Otufe, page 3

Research Question

_____

_____

_____

Central Idea

_____

_____

_____

**Now, look at your research notes. Write a central idea for your own
information report.**

_____

_____

_____

How to Make an Outline

Make an outline for your information report:

- Start with a title that tells what your outline is about.
- Write an introduction that tells your central idea.
- Turn each research question into a main idea, and add details.
- Use Roman numerals for the main ideas and capital letters and numbers for the details.
- Write a conclusion.

How to Make an Outline, continued

Type your outline and paste it here.

Draft Your Information Report

Draft the Introduction

See how this writer reviewed her notes and created a central idea for her report.

> **Notes**
> - Pluto is large enough to be round
> - Pluto orbits the sun
> - If Pluto is a planet, Ceres and Eris have to be planets too
> - Eris is larger than Pluto
> - Pluto is smaller than Earth's moon
> - Pluto doesn't have enough gravity to clear away things that are about its same size
> - Pluto is big enough to have its own moons

> **Central Idea**
> Pluto's status as a planet is debatable.

Now show two ways to draft the title and introduction for the report. Be sure to include the central idea.

1. Try starting with a surprising fact.

_____

_____

_____

_____

_____

_____

2. Try starting with a question that makes a connection to your readers' lives.

_____

_____

_____

_____

_____

_____

Use your outline from pages 123–124 to draft an introduction for your information report. Use your own paper.

© National Geographic Learning, a part of Cengage Learning, Inc.

Draft the Body

See how this writer turned her notes into an outline.

II. Definition of a planet

    A. What is a planet?

        1. no formal definition for many years

            a. used to be defined by common sense

            b. formally defined in 2006

        2. has to orbit the sun

        3. has to be largely spherical

        4. has to have gravity to clear away all other objects around it

        5. other planets like Earth do not always clear away close objects

            a. Pluto can't clear away close objects

            b. neither can some other planets, however

Use this part of the outline above to draft a paragraph for this report.

_____

_____

_____

_____

_____

_____

_____

_____

_____

_____

_____

_____

_____

_____

_____

_____

Now, use your outline from pages 123–124 to draft the body of your own information report. Add it to your introduction.

Draft Your Information Report, continued

Draft the Conclusion

Read this report and add the conclusion.

Is Pluto a Planet?

Pluto is so small that scientists have wondered whether it really is a planet. In 2003 a new object was discovered in our solar system. It was farther away than Pluto. It was larger, too. If Pluto was a planet, this new object had to be one, too.

This new object led to scientists defining what planets are. Planets were not formally defined until 2006. A new definition was made with three criteria. Pluto only meets two. Pluto's gravity cannot clear away close-by objects. But other planets can't clear away all nearby objects either. Many scientists were unsatisfied.

_____

_____

_____

_____

_____

_____

_____

_____

_____

_____

_____

_____

Now use your outline on pages 123 and 124 to draft a conclusion for your own report. Add it to the introduction and body of your report.

Make Source Cards

Locate a book, magazine article, newspaper article, and Web site that you may have used as a source for your report. Record the information here for any of the types of sources you used.

Book

Source #1

Title:

Author:
Publisher:
City:
Year:

Web Site

Source #2

Article or Page Title:

Author:
Web Site Title:
Web Address:

Magazine Article

Source #3

Article Title:

Author:
Magazine:
Issue Date:
Pages:

Newspaper Article

Source #4

Article Title:

Author:
Newspaper:
Issue Date:
Page:

© National Geographic Learning, a part of Cengage Learning, Inc.

Create a Bibliography

Use the information about each source to create a bibliography. List the sources in alphabetical order by the author's last name. Here's how one writer listed her sources.

Book

Source #1
Title: The Sun, Moon,
    and Stars
Author: Dan T. Smith
Publisher: Magnetic Publishing
City: San Francisco
Year: 2013

Web Site

Source #2
Article or Page Title: "The Planets"

Author: Tara Yang
Web Site Title: Planet Watch
Web Address: www.planetwatch.org

Magazine Article

Source #3
Article Title: "Unlocking the Secrets
    of the Solar System"
Author: Barbara Brooks
Magazine: The Star Files
Issue Date: June 2012
Pages: 17-23

Newspaper Article

Source #4
Article Title: "Scientists Debate the
    Nature of Planets"
Author: Frank Mobley
Newspaper: Westfield Ledger
Issue Date: Nov. 25, 2013
Page: B3

Works Cited

_____

_____

_____

_____

_____

_____

_____

_____

Now, create a bibliography for your own information report. Include all the sources you quoted or that you paraphrased. Use your own paper.

Revise an Information Report

Use page 130 to gather feedback for revising and plan what changes you'll make to your paper.

1. Ask one peer to read your paper. Have your reader answer the following questions on a separate sheet of paper.

What to Ask During a Peer Conference

1. Is my introduction interesting?

2. Does my paper have a clear central idea?

3. Does everything in the writing go together?

4. Are there any parts that are confusing or don't belong?

5. What's one thing you wish you could picture more clearly?

2. Now, read their answers and reflect on your work. Answer these questions:

What's the best thing about your report?

_____

_____

How can you make your report more focused and unified?

_____

_____

_____

3. Now you're ready to decide how you will revise your paper. Describe the changes you plan to make.

_____

_____

_____

_____

_____

_____

_____

_____

_____

_____

_____

Revise an Information Report, continued

1. **Evaluate this draft of an information report. What changes are needed?**

_____

_____

_____

_____

_____

Revising Checklist

☐ Is the introduction interesting?

☐ Does the paper have a clear central idea?

☐ Does each main idea relate to the central idea?

☐ Are all source references in the right place?

2. **Revise the draft. Use revising marks to show your changes. Do research to find a few details you can add.**

Revising

MARK	WHAT IT MEANS
∧	Insert something.
↰	Move to here.
⌄	Replace with this.
⸚	Take out.
⁋	Make a new paragraph.

Olympus Mons

Can you imagine a volcano on another planet? Olympus Mons is a volcano on Mars. Its center is 13 miles high. The outside (Gordon 21) is 335 miles wide. The biggest volcano on Earth is in Hawaii. It's called Mauna Loa. Hawaii has lots of other volcanoes too. Over millions of years, eruptions made Olympus Mons bigger. Each eruption released more lava. The layers of lava built up over time. Scientists think Olympus Mons is over one billion years old. No volcanoes on Earth are that old. Volcanic eruptions on Earth are very dangerous.

3. **Now use the checklist to help you revise the draft of your own information report on a clean sheet of paper.**

Edit and Proofread

Grammar Workout: Check Irregular Verbs

**Change the underlined past-tense verbs to their correct form.
Write the sentences.**

1. Before I researched my report, I never <u>knowed</u> the early astronauts <u>eated</u>
freeze-dried foods while in space. _____

_____

2. Neil Armstrong and Buzz Aldrin <u>bringed</u> an American flag with them during
the Apollo 11 mission. _____

_____

3. Armstrong <u>taked</u> a famous photo of Aldrin saluting the flag while on the
surface of the moon. _____

_____

4. After living through the Apollo 13 disaster, astronaut Jim Lovell <u>writed</u> a book
about it called *Lost Moon*. _____

_____

5. In 1995, the book was <u>maked</u> into a movie. _____

_____

Spelling Workout: Check Past-Tense Verbs with *-ed*

Write each verb in the past tense.

1. walk _____	7. look _____	13. fill _____
2. show _____	8. play _____	14. wash _____
3. amuse _____	9. recycle _____	15. exercise _____
4. increase _____	10. save _____	16. unite _____
5. terrify _____	11. satisfy _____	17. bury _____
6. jam _____	12. slip _____	18. prefer _____

© National Geographic Learning, a part of Cengage Learning, Inc.

Edit and Proofread, continued

Mechanics Workout: Check Titles

Rewrite the following sentences to fix mistakes in capitalization and punctuation.

1. Astronomer Dan Smith wrote a book called The sun, moon, and Stars.

_____

2. Smith says, The relationship between the Earth and Mars is fascinating.

_____

3. Samantha searched the magazine The Star Files for an article about Venus.

_____

4. Today's Pleasantville Tribune had an article called Debate about water on Mars

continues. _____

5. The newspaper The Weekly Planet has a headline that reads Martian baby found.

_____

_____

Check Grammar, Spelling, and Mechanics

Proofread the passage. Check the spelling, capitalization, and punctuation, and the form of past-tense verbs. Correct the mistakes.

Revising	
MARK	**WHAT IT MEANS**
∧	Insert something.
↶	Move to here.
⋏	Replace with this.
⸎	Take out.
¶	Make a new paragraph.

In the book What we Know about Space, Dr. Albert Lee writed about the history of people's interest in space.

Ever since people first lookked up and seed the stars, we have wondered about them. We have tryed to find out more through space exploration. The first human beings goed to the moon in 1969. Neil Armstrong is famous for saying, This is one small step for a man, one giant leap for mankind.

Edit and Proofread Your Information Report

Now edit and proofread your work.

Remember to Check

- ☐ irregular verbs
- ☐ past tense verbs with –*ed*
- ☐ titles and quotes
- ☐ _____
- ☐ _____

1. Use a checklist as you edit and proofread.
Add things you are working on to the checklist.

2. Look to see which errors are marked most often.
Jot down your top three trouble spots.

_____

_____

_____

3. Ask your teacher about ways to fix these mistakes, or check out the Grammar Handbook for information.

Focus on Spelling

Improve your spelling by following these steps.

1. Create a personal spelling list. Record words that you misspelled. Look up the correct spelling in the dictionary and add these words to **My Spelling List**.

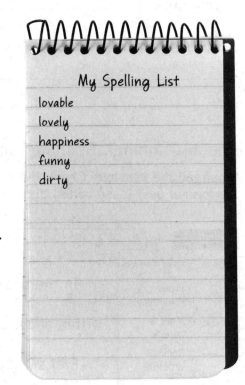

My Spelling List

lovable
lovely
happiness
funny
dirty

2. Pick twelve words. Write six sentences, using two of the words in each sentence. Wacky sentences are just fine! Double-check the spelling of the words. Then write six different sentences, using different pairs of spelling words.

3. Organize your words into lists. List your words in alphabetical order. Next list them by the number of letters. Spell the words aloud as you write them.

4. Make a personal word wall with your spelling words. List your words on chart paper. Read the words on your word wall. Then spell them letter by letter. Next close your eyes and spell them again, letter by letter. Open your eyes. Did you spell the words correctly?

5. Invent a story to help you remember difficult words. For example:
<u>**Word**</u>   cemetery
<u>**Story**</u>   got scared walking through the cemetery and yelled, "e-e-e!" as I ran away. (The word *cemetery* has three e's.)

Publish, Share, and Reflect

Publish and Share Your Information Report

**Check the final format you used to publish your information report.
Then answer the following questions.**

Publishing

What was the final format of your project?	How did you share your project?
☐ Wrote it neatly by hand	☐ Shared it with a large group
☐ Typed it on a computer	☐ Shared it with a small group

1. Whether you published it by hand or on the computer, what did you do to dress up your final product?

_____

_____

_____

_____

2. How did you share your work? What did you learn through sharing your work?

_____

_____

_____

_____

_____

_____

_____

_____

_____

_____

_____

_____

Reflect on Your Information Report

Think about what you did to research and write your information report.

1. What do you like best about your work? _____

_____

_____

2. What did you do well? _____

_____

_____

3. What could you improve about your work? _____

_____

_____

_____

4. What did you learn about yourself while writing? _____

_____

_____

_____

5. How did following the research process help you tell about your topic? _____

_____

_____

6. Decide whether to add your information report to your Writing Portfolio. Explain your decision.

❑ Yes, I will add this to my Writing Portfolio.

_____

_____

❑ No, I will not add this to my Writing Portfolio.

_____

_____

© National Geographic Learning, a part of Cengage Learning, Inc.

Summary Paragraph

Read the article. Then read the two summary paragraphs and answer the questions.

The Little Woman Who Changed the World

by Emma Triches

The fight against slavery took many forms. There were debates in Congress. There were slave revolts. There were anti-slavery writings. Harriet Beecher Stowe fought slavery with her novel, *Uncle Tom's Cabin*. The book tells the story of a slave's life with his masters. It was a success. In fact, it was translated into 37 languages.

Uncle Tom's Cabin made people think about slavery and equal rights. President Lincoln called Harriet "the little woman" who started a "big war." Stowe's book helped people realize the evils of slavery.

Feature Checklist

A good summary paragraph

☐ names the title and author of the work you are summarizing

☐ states the original writer's ideas in your own words

☐ includes the main ideas

☐ leaves out details that are not important.

1. Which summary paragraph is better? Why?

_____

_____

_____

_____

_____

_____

2. How original is the writer's word choice in each summary paragraph?

_____

_____

_____

_____

_____

_____

Summary Paragraphs

A. Emma Triches's article "The Little Woman Who Changed the World" tells about Harriet Beecher Stowe. Stowe wrote a novel about slavery. It was titled *Uncle Tom's Cabin*. The book was very successful and helped the fight against slavery.

B. Emma Triches explains that people fought slavery in many ways. Harriet Beecher Stowe wrote *Uncle Tom's Cabin*. It is the story of a slave's life with his masters. The book was an instant success. In fact, it was translated into 37 languages.

3. What main ideas are missing from the poor summary?

_____

_____

_____

_____

_____

_____

Plan a Summary Paragraph

Use this page to plan your summary paragraph.

1. Read carefully the work you will be summarizing. If you're working with a copy you can mark up, underline or highlight important ideas as you read.

2. If you're working with a copy you can't mark up, use sticky notes to write down your ideas as you read.

3. Fill out a summary planner to begin your writing.

Summary Planner

Title and Author: _____

Topic: _____

Paragraph or Section 1

+

Paragraph or Section 2

+

Paragraph or Section 3

+

Paragraph or Section 4

+

Paragraph or Section 5

=

Summary of Selection: _____

_____

_____

_____

_____

Draft a Summary Paragraph

Use your Summary Planner from page 138 to try a couple of different drafts of your summary paragraph.

Drafting Checklist

- ☐ Include the title and author of the work you are summarizing.
- ☐ State the original writer's ideas in your own words.
- ☐ Include main ideas and important details.
- ☐ Leave out details that are not important.

Draft 1

_____

_____

_____

_____

_____

_____

_____

_____

_____

Draft 2

_____

_____

_____

_____

_____

_____

_____

_____

_____

_____

Revise a Summary Paragraph

1. Use the checklist to evaluate this draft of a summary paragraph. What changes are needed?

_____

_____

_____

_____

_____

2. Revise the draft. Use revising marks to show your changes.

Revising

MARK	WHAT IT MEANS
∧	Insert something.
↶	Move to here.
⌐	Replace with this.
⸎	Take out.
¶	Make a new paragraph.

The Underground Railroad

Daniel Schulman's *Escaping to Freedom* is about the Underground Railroad. It was not an actual railroad. It was a set of paths slaves traveled on. Along the Underground Railroad, there were many extremely thoughtful and helpful people. They helped shelter the slaves. They also provided them with food and water. They gave them clothing too. Traveling on the Underground Railroad was difficult. Slaves had to travel hundreds and hundreds of miles to get to safety. The trip took months. Sometimes it took years. Some slaves never made it to freedom.

3. Choose one of the drafts of your summary paragraph on page 139. Use the checklist to help you revise it.

© National Geographic Learning, a part of Cengage Learning, Inc.

Edit and Proofread

Grammar Workout: Check Subject and Object Pronouns

Replace the underlined word or words with the correct pronoun. Then write the new sentence.

1. <u>Josiah</u> was taken from his family when <u>Josiah</u> was only a child.

_____

2. <u>Josiah's</u> name was given to <u>Josiah</u> by his first master.

_____

3. <u>The plantation</u> was the place where <u>Josiah and the other slaves</u> worked.

_____

4. <u>Josiah</u> heard <u>the men</u> discuss a plan to sell <u>Josiah.</u>

_____

5. <u>Josiah</u> loved his wife and didn't want to leave <u>his wife.</u>

_____

6. <u>Josiah's wife</u> and <u>Josiah</u> planned to run away together.

_____

Spelling Workout: Check Words Ending in y

Add -s, -ed, or -ing to the verb in parentheses to complete each sentence.

1. Josiah _____ on the money he earned to buy freedom. **(rely)**

2. Josiah was _____ to save money. **(try)**

3. At that time, Josiah _____ in Indiana. **(stay)**

4. Schulman's book effectively _____ how hard Josiah's life was. **(convey)**

5. When Josiah was a slave, he _____ Riley's every command. **(obey)**

6. He began _____ farther and farther from the farmhouse. **(stray)**

Mechanics Workout: Check Capitalization of Proper Nouns

Use proofreading marks to correct the capitalization errors in each sentence.

1. The kentucky anti-slavery society helped Henson and others in their fight for freedom.

2. Thanks to the underground railroad, many slaves could find freedom.

3. Slavery was among the issues that sparked the civil war.

4. The army of the North was known as the grand army of the republic, or GAR.

5. The period that followed the war is called reconstruction.

Check Grammar, Spelling, and Mechanics

Proofread the passage. Check the spelling and the use of pronouns and the capitalization of proper nouns. Correct the mistakes.

Editing and Proofreading Marks	
∧	Insert something.
⋏	Add a comma.
⩘	Add a semicolon.
⊙	Add a period.
⊙	Add a colon.
ᵛᵛ ᵛᵛ	Add quotation marks.
ᵛ	Add an apostrophe.
≡	Capitalize.
/	Make lower case.
℘	Delete.
¶	Make new paragraph.
◯	Check spelling.
⌒	Replace with this.
∿	Change order.
#	Insert space.
⌒	Close up.

Harriet Tubman was born a slave before the civil war. When Harriet was 30, he decided to escape. She wanted to go to the North and be free. She settled in Pennsylvania. She founded an effective anti-slavery organization.

The underground railroad helped more than 100,000 slaves find freedom. The underground railroad was not a real railroad. Instead, they was a network of people against slavery. Them supplyed runaway slaves with a place to hide.

Edit and Proofread, continued

Edit and Proofread Your Summary Paragraph

Now edit and proofread your work.

Remember to Check

☐ subject and object pronouns
☐ words ending in y
☐ capitalization of proper nouns
☐ _____
☐ _____

1. Use a checklist as you edit and proofread. Add things you are working on to the checklist.

2. Look to see which errors are marked most often. Jot down your top three trouble spots.

_____

_____

3. Ask your teacher about ways to fix these mistakes, or check out the Grammar Handbook for information.

Focus on Spelling

Improve your spelling by following these steps.

1. Create a personal spelling list. Record words that you misspelled. Look up the correct spelling in the dictionary and add these words to **My Spelling List**.

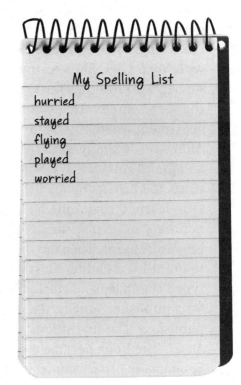

My Spelling List
hurried
stayed
flying
played
worried

2. Pick twelve words. Write each word four times. First, write it in all lowercase letters. Next, write it in all capital letters. After that, write the vowels in lowercase and the consonants in uppercase. Last, write the word using fancy letters that you create on your own.

3. Work with a partner to play **I'm Thinking of a Spelling Word**. Take turns giving each other clues. Some clues might be *I'm thinking of a word that rhymes with . . .* or *I'm thinking of a word that means . . .* With each clue, the answer should include the word and its spelling.

4. Work with a partner to play a scrambled-letter game. Take each other's spelling words and write them in scrambled form. See if your partner can unscramble them.

5. Use an audio recorder and record your words and their spelling. Then listen to your recording, checking to see that you spelled each word correctly.

Cause-and-Effect Essay

This cause-and-effect essay has some problems. Read the essay and answer the questions.

The Publication of Anne Frank's Diary

by Chris Quinley

Anne Frank died in a concentration camp in March 1945. Frank's sister Margot also died at the camp. Their father, Otto, had found freedom a month before. He was in a different concentration camp. Otto did not know about the death of Anne and Margot. So he went to Amsterdam, hoping to find his daughters.

Otto spent months looking for his daughters. He finally learned the truth from an eyewitness. He also met with Miep Gies. She was the Dutch woman who hid the Frank family in the secret annex. That was the small apartment where Anne's family hid. After Anne's family was arrested, Miep had found Anne's diary. She gave the pages to Otto. As he read the diary, Otto learned that Anne had wanted her diary to be published. At first, he was hesitant. Then, he decided to grant his daughter's last wish. He typed the diary and started looking for a publisher. Finally, the diary was published. The first title was *The Secret Annex*. The book became a success. Soon, many other countries were translating and publishing it.

From that day, Otto Frank traveled the world to tell his daughter's story. His mission was to work toward peace and freedom. Anne's wish was fulfilled. Her story is read all over the world.

Feature Checklist

A good cause-and-effect essay

- ☐ has an introduction with a clear main idea
- ☐ has a body that explains the causes and effects in detail
- ☐ has a conclusion that sums up the main ideas and leaves you with something to think about.

1. **How could the beginning be improved?**

_____

_____

_____

_____

2. **Is the chain of causes and effects clear? Explain.**

_____

_____

_____

_____

3. **Does this essay have a strong conclusion? Explain.**

_____

_____

_____

_____

_____

_____

_____

_____

Cause-and-Effect Essay, continued

This cause-and-effect essay is a good model. What makes it good? Read the essay and answer the questions.

The Anne Frank House
by Jordan Lewis

Anne Frank's diary inspired readers around the world. Anne's story became so popular that the house where she and her family hid is now a museum. It is called the Anne Frank House. The Anne Frank House is not only a museum, though. It is a place dedicated to tolerance and freedom.

The museum opened in 1960. It shows visitors where Anne hid with her family. It also displays pages from Anne's diary. However, the owners of the museum realized they could do much more. As a result, they started a project called Understanding Diversity. In this project, ten schools from all over the world work together. The project's goal is to create an online exhibit about immigration. Students conduct interviews, give class presentations, and share suggestions via e-mail. They live far away from each other, so they use a Web site to share information. By working together, they learn a lot about one another's cultures. By researching the experiences of immigrants, they learn tolerance. Thanks to Understanding Diversity, tolerance and freedom are promoted.

Anne Frank died very young. However, her story is not forgotten. The Anne Frank House is still spreading Anne's message of freedom. Thanks to the Anne Frank House, tragedies like the Holocaust are less likely to happen again.

Feature Checklist

A good cause-and-effect essay

☐ has an introduction with a clear main idea

☐ has a body that explains the causes and effects in detail

☐ has a conclusion that sums up the main ideas and leaves you with something to think about.

4. **What is the main idea of the essay? Is the main idea clearly stated in the introduction and in the conclusion?**

_____

_____

_____

_____

_____

5. **How does the author make causes and effects clear?**

_____

_____

_____

_____

_____

6. **What is good about the conclusion?**

_____

_____

_____

_____

_____

Use Graphic Organizers

The box below contains events from the story "Before We Were Free." Some of these events are causes, and some are effects. Read the events. Then fill in the graphic organizer to match each cause with its effect.

Events

- Anita and her mother go into hiding.
- The SIM come into the house where Anita and Mami are hiding.
- Anita and Mami are flown to New York City.
- Anita's father and uncle are arrested.
- Anita and Mami hide in the crawl space.
- Mami tells Anita about her work with the Butterflies.
- Anita feels proud of Mami.
- Paratroopers find Anita and Mami.

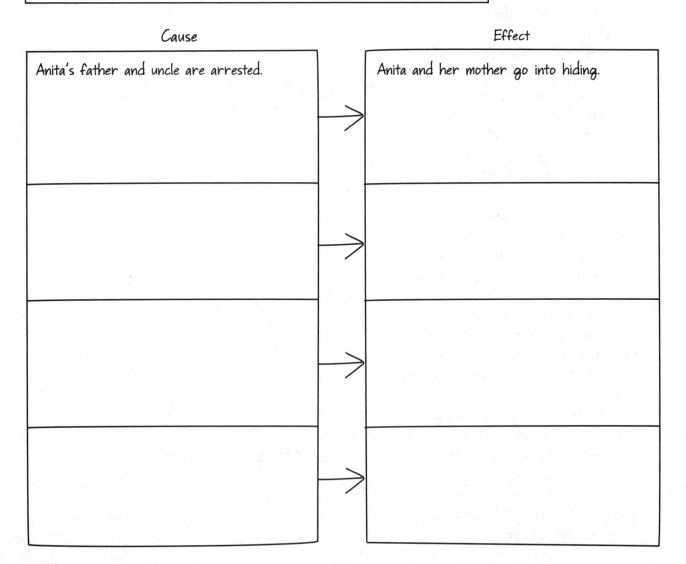

Cause

Effect

Anita's father and uncle are arrested.

Anita and her mother go into hiding.

Use Graphic Organizers, continued

The box below contains events from the selection "Escaping to Freedom."
Read the events. Then fill in the cause-and-effect chain organizer to put the
events in order.

Events

· Josiah Henson made a plan to escape slavery.

· The Underground Railroad led the Henson family to freedom in Canada.

· Josiah Henson learned that his owner planned to sell him.

· The Henson family left Kentucky with the help of the Underground Railroad.

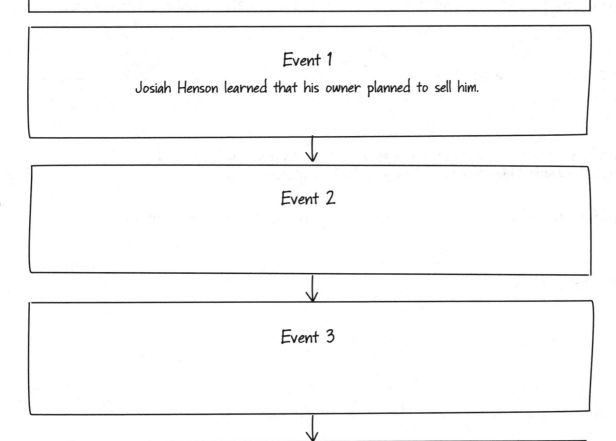

Event 1

Josiah Henson learned that his owner planned to sell him.

↓

Event 2

↓

Event 3

↓

Event 4

**Look at the events in your cause-and-effect chain. What main point can you
make about the events in the chain?**

_____

_____

How to Write a Good Introduction

Identify which topic sentence best fits the central idea. Label that sentence "just right." Then, explain why the others do not fit.

Central Idea: I want to write about Nelson Mandela's fight for freedom.

Topic Sentences:

1. Nelson Mandela and F. W. de Klerk both received the Nobel Prize for Peace because of their work to end apartheid in South Africa. _____

_____

2. Nelson Mandela fought for many years for freedom in South Africa and eventually won.

_____

3. Many people think Nelson Mandela is a great man. _____

_____

Read each central idea and write your own topic sentence for it. You may need to research the central idea before writing your topic sentence.

4. Central Idea: I want to write about women gaining the right to vote in America.

> Topic Sentence

4. Central Idea: I want to write about the March on Washington in 1963.

> Topic Sentence

How to Link Causes and Effects

Revise this cause-and-effect essay. Add transition
words (from the box or your own) to signal causes
and effects.

TRANSITION WORDS		
because	so	due to
since	it follows that	as a result
therefore	the effect was	thus

Freedom Fighters

There are some countries in the world where women have to fight for their

freedom. Afghanistan is one of those countries. For years, leaders prevented

women from attending schools. Women were missing out on an education. They

weren't allowed to work, either. Some women in Afghanistan decided to make a

change.

A group of women formed RAWA in 1977. RAWA stands for Revolutionary

Association of the Women of Afghanistan. This group believes that women and

men should have equal rights. They hold demonstrations. They also publish a

monthly newsletter. These activities help them fight for equal rights.

The members of RAWA think things are improving. The government that was

taking away women's rights was overthrown. The attitudes of many leaders

changed. But RAWA believes that there is still work to be done. There are still

places where people are not treated equally. Women there must keep fighting for

freedom.

The work that groups like RAWA do is important Everyone deserves freedom.

People around the world should help these groups fight for women's rights.

How to Finish Strong

Read the first two paragraphs of the cause-and-effect essay.
Then add a strong conclusion to make the essay more effective.

Equal Rights

Most people believe that all Americans should have equal rights. However, this wasn't always the case. In the past, African Americans were not seen as equals by some. The actions of many brave people changed this. These people fought hard for their beliefs. As a result, African Americans won equal rights.

Several years ago, some laws discriminated against African Americans. Because of these laws, African Americans were kept out of many schools, restaurants, and public places. They were not allowed to have certain jobs. Many could not vote. Very few were elected to public office. There were also some cases of violence against African Americans. Events like these caused a fight for civil rights. Leaders like Martin Luther King, Jr., fought for equality. They organized boycotts and demonstrations. Because of their efforts, people started protesting. Their protests were usually peaceful. Some people stopped riding buses. They held marches and rallies. Because they believed in equality, they did not stop until the unfair laws were changed.

_____

_____

_____

_____

_____

_____

_____

_____

_____

_____

_____

_____

_____

_____

Plan a Cause-and-Effect Essay

Use pages 151–152 to plan your cause-and-effect essay.

1. Choose a topic for your cause-and-effect essay. In the left column of the chart, record names of people who fought for freedom. In the right column, explain what caused each person to fight for freedom. Circle the topic you choose.

Person	Cause

2. Now decide the most important thing you want to say about your topic. This is the central idea of your essay. Write your central idea on the lines below.

_____

_____

_____

_____

_____

3. Use a cause-and-effect chain to organize your ideas. In the first box, put the first event. Then, list the first effect from that event. In the next box, list the next effect, and so on.

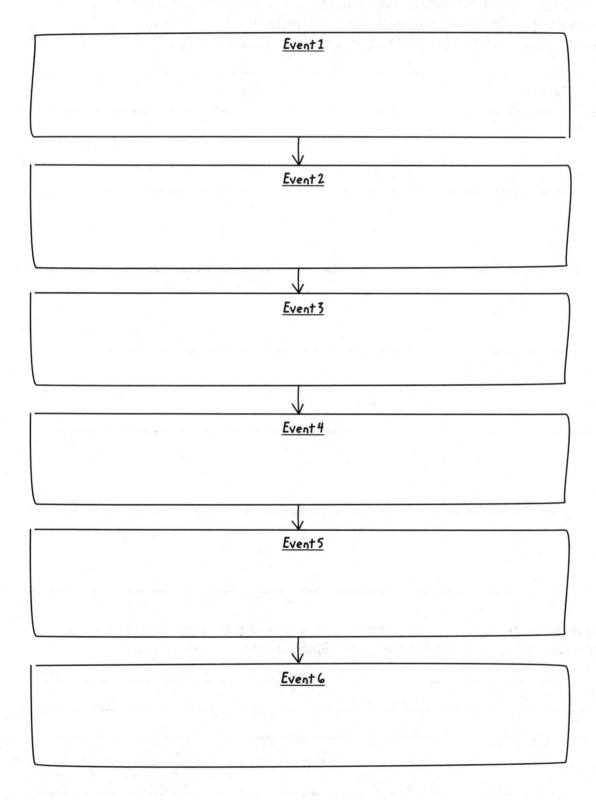

Draft a Cause-and-Effect Essay

Use your plan from pages 151–152 to write the first draft of your cause-and-effect essay.

Drafting Checklist

- ☐ Start with a good introduction that contains a clear main idea.
- ☐ Explain each cause and effect in detail.
- ☐ Tell about real events in the order they happened.
- ☐ Use transition words to link causes and effects.
- ☐ Sum up the main idea in the essay's conclusion.
- ☐ Leave the reader with something to think about.

_____

_____

_____

_____

_____

_____

_____

_____

_____

_____

_____

_____

_____

_____

_____

_____

_____

_____

_____

_____

_____

Revise a Cause-and-Effect Essay

1. Use the checklist to evaluate this draft of a cause-and-effect essay. What changes are needed?

_____

_____

_____

_____

_____

Revising Checklist
☐ Did you include a general statement of your main point?
☐ Are the causes and effects clear?
☐ Can you add any cause-and-effect words to improve flow?
☐ Could you consolidate or delete any ideas or details?

2. Revise the draft. Use revising marks to show your changes.

Revising	
MARK	**WHAT IT MEANS**
∧	Insert something.
↶	Move to here.
⌐	Replace with this.
⤴	Take out.
⁋	Make a new paragraph.

Winning the Right to Vote

Can you imagine a time when women were not allowed to vote? Ninety years ago, only men had the right to vote. Crusaders like Susan B. Anthony wanted to change that. Women wanted an equal voice.

Anthony helped form the National American Woman Suffrage Association. The group worked to convince the government to give women the right to vote. They staged protests and speeches. This helped them gain public support.

Women won the right to vote in 1920. Woodrow Wilson was president. This moment changed history. Now men and women have an equal voice.

3. Now use the checklist to help you revise the draft of your cause-and-effect essay on pages 153–154.

Edit and Proofread

Grammar Workout: Check Reflexive and Intensive Pronouns

Use a reflexive or intensive pronoun to complete each sentence.

1. Brittany sat by _____ after history class thinking about freedom.

2. The teacher, Mr. DeSouza, asked _____ if he should disturb Brittany.

3. But soon Brittany said, "I believe in _____. I am free to be anything I want to be."

4. "I think all my classmates should tell _____ that, too."

5. "I agree," said Mr. DeSouza. "If you set good goals for _____ you can do anything!"

Spelling Workout: Check Words with *q* or *ei*

Find and correct the misspelled words in the following paragraph.

> That bus driver in Montgomery, Alabama, probably thought it was going to be another normal day in the nieghborhood. But this day would be qiute different. Rosa Parks got on his bus, and she was one tough lady. The bus filled up qiuckly; all the seats got taken. Then another rider, a white man, got on. The driver asked Rosa to give up her seat. Rosa was not happy to recieve that request. She said "no." The driver couldn't beleive it. He stopped the bus in the middle of traffic. He called the police. Rosa was determined to resist. She waited qiuetly for the police.

Edit and Proofread, continued

Mechanics Workout: Check Commas

Use proofreading marks to correct the errors with commas.

1. Kim's history class was learning about Rosa Parks Martin Luther King, Jr., and Thurgood Marshall.

2. Her teacher had the class do research about the people in books, articles and online.

3. The students looked for interviews speeches and documentaries.

4. Kim even asked her grandma aunt, and parents what they knew about these famous people.

5. She found some interesting quotes, drawings and, photographs to add to her report.

Check Grammar, Spelling, and Mechanics

Proofread the passage. Check the spelling and use of pronouns and commas. Correct the mistakes.

Editing and Proofreading Marks	
∧	Insert something.
⩘	Add a comma.
⩘	Add a semicolon.
⊙	Add a period.
⊙	Add a colon.
⩛ ⩛	Add quotation marks.
⩛	Add an apostrophe.
≡	Capitalize.
/	Make lower case.
℘	Delete.
¶	Make new paragraph.
◯	Check spelling.
⌒	Replace with this.
∿	Change order.
#	Insert space.
⌒	Close up.

Today we recieved an assignment in history class. We have to write an essay. Although ieght of my freinds groaned about it, I herself am very excited. I love history!

I am going to write my paper about Martin Luther King, Jr. I think he was a good leader minister, speaker and father. There is no qeustion about his importance in our history. I wonder if Dr. King really knew how much he gave of hisself to improve people's rights. His "I Have a Dream" speech is qiute famous. The speech it changed a lot of people's minds.

Edit and Proofread Your Cause-and-Effect Essay

Now edit and proofread your work.

Remember to Check

- [ ] reflexive and intensive pronouns
- [ ] spelling of words with *q* or *ei*
- [ ] serial commas
- [ ] _____
- [ ] _____

1. Use a checklist as you edit and proofread. Add things you are working on to the checklist.

2. Look to see which errors are marked most often. Jot down your top three trouble spots.

_____

_____

_____

3. Ask your teacher about ways to fix these mistakes, or check out the Grammar Handbook for information.

Focus on Spelling

Improve your spelling by following these steps.

1. Create a personal spelling list. Record words that you misspelled. Look up the correct spelling in the dictionary and add these words to **My Spelling List**.

2. Pick twelve words. Make a colorful display of the words. Get a sheet of chart paper. Write each word three times in a different color.

3. Work with a partner to play **Spelling Tic-Tac-Toe**. Draw a tic-tac-toe grid. Take turns asking each other to spell words. When a player spells a word correctly, that player gets to mark an X or an O on the game board.

4. Write the letters for each word on separate squares of paper. Attach the letters for each word to each other with a paper clip. Unscramble the letters to spell each of your words.

5. Invent your own memory strategy for difficult words. Think of a good way to remember why a word is spelled a certain way. For example:

Word	Explanation
dessert	"It has two s's for <u>s</u>weet <u>s</u>tuff!"

Publish, Share, and Reflect

Publish and Share Your Cause-and-Effect Essay

**Check the final formats you used to publish your cause-and-effect essay.
Then answer the following questions.**

Publishing

What was the final format of your project?	How did you share your project?
☐ Wrote it neatly by hand	☐ Shared it with a large group
☐ Typed it on a computer	☐ Shared it with a small group

1. Whether you published it by hand or on the computer, what did you do to dress up your final project?

_____

_____

_____

_____

_____

2. How did you share your work? What did you learn through sharing your work?

_____

_____

_____

_____

_____

_____

_____

_____

_____

_____

_____

_____

Reflect on Your Cause-and-Effect Essay

Read your cause-and-effect essay. Then answer questions 1–6.

1. What do you like best about your work? _____

_____

_____

2. What did you do well? _____

_____

_____

3. What could you improve about your work? _____

_____

_____

_____

4. Did you show why the person you wrote about was important? _____

_____

_____

5. How can you work on improving organization? _____

_____

_____

6. Will you add your cause-and-effect essay to your Writing Portfolio? Explain
your decision.

❑ Yes, I will add this to my Writing Portfolio.

_____

_____

❑ No, I will not add this to my Writing Portfolio.

_____

_____

Speech

What makes this speech a good model?
Read the speech and answer the questions.

Feature Checklist

A good speech

☐ makes and defends an argument

☐ presents its points in a clear and organized way

☐ stays focused and on topic

☐ wraps up its argument in a strong conclusion

Why We Should Study Astronomy

by Cal Perry

Have you ever wondered how people got around before maps and GPS? They had their own kind of map: the stars. They passed on what they learned from the stars from generation to generation. These days, however, people don't spend much time studying the stars, and I think that is a mistake.

Even though we have many modern ways of getting around, the stars could still help us in a crisis. If the power went out, people could use the stars to find their direction. If a ship's navigation system failed, the stars could help its captain find land. However, the stars can only help us if we know what they are telling us.

I also believe that learning about the stars helps people to make sense of the universe. The world is a huge place, and that can be frightening. Studying the stars helps us see our place in the universe, and understand how it works. As the authors of the book *21st Century Astronomy* point out, people don't only learn by memorizing facts. They also learn by noticing patterns in the world. The stars follow patterns that we can observe over time.

1. **How does the beginning get the listeners' attention?**

_____

_____

_____

_____

_____

2. **What claim does the writer make?**

_____

_____

_____

_____

_____

_____

3. **What evidence does the writer give to support his claim in this section?**

_____

_____

_____

_____

_____

_____

_____

Learning about the stars also helps us connect to our history as human beings. The stars help us understand our past and our culture. They help us see how it felt to look up at the sky during a different time in history. For example, by learning about the stars, we can learn new things about the Underground Railroad. According to the National Aeronautics and Space Administration (NASA) website, people escaping slavery in the Underground Railroad used the stars to map a path to freedom. A song from back then, called "Follow the Drinking Gourd" tells how they used the Big Dipper to find their way.

The entire world around us may change, but at any moment we can look up and see what people saw hundreds of years ago. By looking at the stars, we can learn important lessons about ourselves. In closing, I hope that I have shown how learning about the stars is important to understanding our past, our present, and our future. Let's make sure we continue to pass on this knowledge to future generations.

4. How does the writer use credible sources in this section?

_____

_____

_____

_____

_____

_____

5. How does the writer use the story of the drinking gourd to make his ideas convincing?

_____

_____

_____

_____

_____

_____

6. What is good about the ending?

_____

_____

_____

_____

_____

_____

_____

Evaluate for Development of Ideas

Read each speech. Use the rubric on page 164 to score it for development of ideas. Explain your scores.

Writing Sample 1

Let's Celebrate Our Space History

Back in the 1960s, many of our local companies and workers helped build space equipment. This is a proud part of our history and I think our town museum should have a show to honor their work.

Many photos from that time period have never been seen. Having them in a museum would give kids today a chance to connect with our town's proud past. It would also give those who worked on the program a chance to speak about their experiences. Finally, putting on a show like this would raise money for the museum. It would not be expensive to put on, but it would get many visitors.

Score	1	2	3	4

Writing Sample 2

We Need Astronomy Education

If we want to give our kids a complete education, we must teach them about the stars. Learning about the stars is important and our school has to realize this.

Many kids think math is difficult, and I agree. I think it's one of the toughest subjects. When people study the stars, they use math. Therefore, studying the stars could make math more fun.

Score	1	2	3	4

Writing Rubric

Development of Ideas

	How thoughtful and interesting is the writing?	How well are the ideas or claims explained and supported?
4 Wow!	The writing engages the reader with meaningful ideas or claims and presents them in a way that is interesting and appropriate to the audience, purpose, and type of writing.	The ideas or claims are fully explained and supported. • The ideas or claims are well developed with important details, evidence, and/or description. • The writing feels complete, and the reader is satisfied.
3 Ahh.	<u>Most</u> of the writing engages the reader with meaningful ideas or claims and presents them in a way that is interesting and appropriate to the audience, purpose, and type of writing.	<u>Most</u> of the ideas or claims are explained and supported. • Most of the ideas or claims are developed with important details, evidence, and/or description. • The writing feels mostly complete, but the reader still has some questions.
2 Hmm.	<u>Some</u> of the writing engages the reader with meaningful ideas or claims and presents them in a way that is interesting and appropriate to the audience, purpose, and type of writing.	<u>Some</u> of the ideas or claims are explained and supported. • Only some of the ideas or claims are developed. Details, evidence, and/or description, are limited or not relevant. • The writing leaves the reader with many questions.
1 Huh?	The writing does <u>not</u> engage the reader. It is not appropriate to the audience, purpose, and type of writing.	The ideas or claims are <u>not</u> explained or supported. The ideas lack details, evidence, and/or description, and the writing leaves the reader unsatisfied.

Raise the Score

1. Use the rubric on page 164 to evaluate and score this speech.

Score	1	2	3	4

A New Planetarium

Last week our town council had a meeting about what to do with the old movie theater building on Smith Street. Hey guys, let's turn this movie theater into a planetarium!

The building has been standing since the 1920s. Back then, people didn't have TVs. They went to the movies for fun. Though the building has not been used for many years, it is still strong. According to the City Department of Buildings, it is safe to use. For this reason, I think it would be a waste to tear it down. The building would make a perfect planetarium because it has a high, curved ceiling. It already has plenty of seats for visitors.

Some people might ask why we need a planetarium. It's because we live in the city. We need a planetarium more than people who live in the country.

In conclusion, I believe a planetarium would be great for people in our community. Let's give our citizens a chance to look to the stars.

2. Explain what the writer should do to raise the score.

_____

_____

_____

_____

_____

_____

_____

_____

3. Now revise the speech on page 165 to improve its style and development of ideas. Write your revised speech here.

Prove it

Look at the photo below and read the bare-bones speech beside it. Then use the "Ways to Prove It" box to help enrich the speech.

Next week, we will be able to see a lunar eclipse from our town. I believe that it is important to set up a town viewing to make sure everyone has a chance to experience it.

First of all, having a town viewing will help everyone see the eclipse safely.

_____
_____
_____
_____
_____
_____
_____
_____
_____
_____
_____
_____
_____
_____
_____

Organize Your Ideas

Plan your speech by filling in a claim and three pieces of evidence in the graphic organizer. In each Evidence box, write a signal word you could use to transition to that evidence.

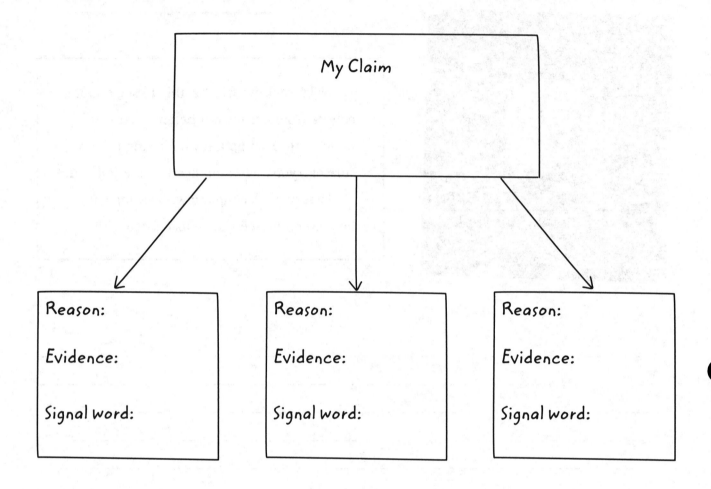

My Claim

Reason:

Evidence:

Signal word:

Reason:

Evidence:

Signal word:

Reason:

Evidence:

Signal word:

Write the first part of your speech. Present your claim and the most important reason and piece of evidence. Include appropriate signal words to clarify the relationship between your ideas.

_____

_____

_____

_____

_____

_____

_____

Plan a Speech

Use pages 169–170 to plan your speech.

1. Gather Evidence

Once you have a claim, you have to gather evidence and support it with credible sources. Write your evidence in the chart below. Show how you will use credible sources to make your argument more convincing. Do some research for this, using print and online resources.

Chart

My Claim:	
Why I Think So:	
Evidence that supports my claim:	

2. Plan How Your Ideas Will Flow

Think about the best way to organize your speech. In what order will you present your evidence? What words will you use to show the connection between pieces of evidence? Use the diagram below to organize the order of your ideas and the words you will use to connect them to your claim.

Claim: _____

_____

Evidence 1: _____

_____

_____

_____

_____

Evidence 2: _____

_____

_____

_____

_____

Evidence 3: _____

_____

_____

_____

© National Geographic Learning, a part of Cengage Learning, Inc.

Draft a Speech

Use your plan from pages 169–170 to write the first draft of your speech.

Drafting Checklist

- ☐ Makes a clear claim.
- ☐ Supports the claim with evidence.
- ☐ Uses a credible source or sources.
- ☐ Wraps up its argument in a strong conclusion.

_____

_____

_____

_____

_____

_____

_____

_____

_____

_____

_____

_____

_____

_____

_____

_____

_____

_____

_____

_____

_____

_____

_____

_____

_____

_____

_____

_____

_____

_____

_____
_____
_____
_____
_____
_____
_____
_____
_____
_____
_____
_____
_____
_____
_____
_____
_____
_____
_____
_____
_____
_____
_____
_____
_____
_____
_____

© National Geographic Learning, a part of Cengage Learning, Inc.

Revise a Speech

1. Use the checklist to evaluate this draft of a speech. What changes are needed?

_____

_____

_____

_____

_____

Revising Checklist

- ☐ Does the introduction get the listeners' attention?
- ☐ Is there enough evidence?
- ☐ Is the style appropriate?
- ☐ Are sentences and paragraphs concise?
- ☐ Are there any unimportant details you could delete?

2. Revise the draft. Use revising marks to show your changes.

Revising

MARK	WHAT IT MEANS
∧	Insert something.
↶	Move to here.
⌐	Replace with this.
ℐ	Take out.
¶	Make a new paragraph.

A New Stargazing Tower

Last year, after a big storm, the lighthouse in our town was moved inland. Since then, the town has been like, what should we do with this? I believe that we should install a telescope in the lighthouse and turn it into a stargazing tower.

The lighthouse was built in 1830 and it is painted red and white. It would make a great stargazing tower. It is the tallest building in our town. It fits 10 people inside the upper deck. According to local astronomy professor Mark Lyon, many stars can be seen from the lighthouse. He noted that the college is willing to donate a telescope.

3. Now use the checklist to help you revise the draft of your speech on pages 171–172.

Edit and Proofread

Grammar Workout: Check Possessive Adjectives

Grammar Workout: Check Possessive Adjectives

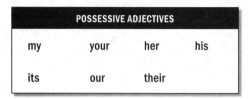

POSSESSIVE ADJECTIVES			
my	your	her	his
its	our	their	

1. Jack Lamont stood at the deck of _____ boat at sunset.

2. He loved the colors _____ rays made across the sky.

3. Jack's wife joined him to look for _____ favorite constellations.

4. She imagined lines connecting the stars to form _____ shapes.

5. "Look to _____ left," she said to Jack. Doesn't that look like a bear?"

Spelling Workout: Check Multisyllabic Words

Find and correct the misspelled words in the following paragraph.

Our class is planing a trip to the Air and Space Museum. I'm so hapy! My dad is a pillot and has taught me a lot about airplanes. But on the trip, I'll actually get to see some of the very first airplanes. And I bellieve that the museum guides will give us all the dettails about the first space shutles. I can't wait for next week!

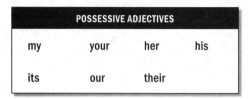

Edit and Proofread, continued

Mechanics Workout: Check Apostrophes in Possessives

Edit each sentence by adding or deleting apostrophes where necessary.

1. Last week, we went to my grandparents house.

2. Usually, my sister's and I get bored there.

3. But this time, the familys' plan was to visit the planetarium.

4. The planetariums films and exhibits were amazing.

5. Now I know a lot more about the planets shapes and sizes.

6. And I learned that our galaxys name is the Milky Way.

Check Grammar, Spelling, and Mechanics

Proofread the passage. Correct errors in spelling and use of possessive adjectives and apostrophes. Correct the mistakes.

Editing and Proofreading Marks	
∧	Insert something.
⋏	Add a comma.
⋏	Add a semicolon.
⊙	Add a period.
⊙	Add a colon.
ᵛ ᵛ	Add quotation marks.
ᵛ	Add an apostrophe.
≡	Capitalize.
/	Make lower case.
℘	Delete.
⁋	Make new paragraph.
⬭	Check spelling.
⌒	Replace with this.
∿	Change order.
#	Insert space.
⌣	Close up.

Last year, their dad and I went camping. We went far away from our citys' lights. We didn't realize it at the time, but it was the year for a lunar eclipse! That night, at least at first, the moons glow filed our campsite. But then his light started to disappear. It beccame so dark out, we couldn't see our hands in front of its faces! Thank goodness for Moms' reminder to always take the flashlights!

Edit and Proofread Your Speech

Now edit and proofread your work.

Remember to Check

☐ possessive adjectives
☐ spelling of multisyllabic words
☐ apostrophes in possessives
☐ _____
☐ _____

1. Use a checklist as you edit and proofread. Add things you are working on to the checklist.

2. Look to see which errors are marked most often. Jot down your top three trouble spots.

_____

_____

_____

3. Ask your teacher about ways to fix these mistakes, or check out the Grammar Handbook for information.

Focus on Spelling

Improve your spelling by following these steps.

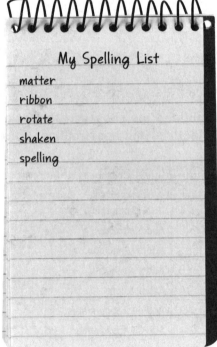

1. Create a personal spelling list. Record words that you misspelled. Look up the correct spelling in the dictionary and add these words to **My Spelling List**.

2. Pick twelve words. Write each word in one color. Then trace it four more times in four different colors. Say each letter to yourself as you trace it.

3. Work with a partner to play **Spelling Catch**. Pitch words to each other by saying, "Here's the pitch! The word is . . ." Take turns pitching. The first "batter" to spell ten words correctly wins.

4. Write each spelling word three times. The first time, just write the word. The second time, write it and circle all the consonants. The third time, write it and circle all the vowels.

5. Play **Memory**. Write each spelling word on two different index cards. Mix up the cards and place them face down. Turn the cards over two at a time. Your goal is to find matching cards. Say and spell the words on the cards you turn over. If you make a match, remove those cards from the game until all the cards are gone.

Publish, Share, and Reflect

Publish and Share Your Speech

Check the final formats you used to publish your speech. Then answer the following questions.

Publishing

What was the final format of your project?	How did you share your project?
☐ Wrote it neatly by hand	☐ Shared it with a large group
☐ Typed it on a computer	☐ Shared it with a small group

1. Whether you published it by hand or on the computer, what did you do to dress up your final project?

_____

_____

_____

_____

2. How did you share your work? What did you learn through sharing your work?

_____

_____

_____

_____

_____

_____

_____

_____

_____

_____

_____

_____

_____

Reflect on Your Speech
Read your speech. Then answer questions 1–6.

1. What do you like best about your work? _____

_____

_____

2. What did you do well? _____

_____

_____

3. What could you improve about your work? _____

_____

_____

_____

4. Does your speech present a convincing argument? _____

_____

_____

5. What was hard about writing this speech? What came easily? _____

_____

_____

_____

_____

6. Will you add your speech to your Writing Portfolio? Explain your decision.

❏ Yes, I will add this to my Writing Portfolio.

_____

_____

❏ No, I will not add this to my Writing Portfolio.

_____

_____

Persuasive Business Letter

What makes this persuasive business letter a good model? Read the letter and answer the questions.

4242 Cloud Dr.
Sunnyville, TN 34271
February 16, 2014

Mr. Simon Aldridge
Midvale Middle School
214 Main St.
Sunnyville, TN 34271

Dear Principal Aldridge:

    For Earth Day, our social studies class has been asked to think of ideas that will help Earth. I think the school should adopt my idea to turn off all inside and outside school lights at 9 p.m.

    This change would help the environment because it saves the electricity that runs the lights. According to the Department of Energy, it takes 2.1 pounds of coal to make one kilowatt of electricity. If we save electricity, we don't have to burn as much coal or other resources.

    Turning off lights also saves money. The electric company's website says that the actual savings depends on the type of light bulbs, but using less electricity means spending less money.

    Mr. Edwards, our science teacher, also says that turning off outdoor lights is better for local wildlife and people who like to watch the night sky.

    There are many reasons to turn off our school lights at night and I suggest that we do.

Sincerely,
Jerome Martin
Jerome Martin

Feature Checklist

A good persuasive business letter

- includes the date, a greeting and closing, and the writer's and reader's addresses
- clearly states what you want the reader to do
- gives two to four supporting reasons
- backs up reasons with facts and evidence
- uses a formal, respectful tone.

1. What is the writer trying to persuade Mr. Aldridge to do?

_____

_____

_____

_____

_____

_____

2. List two reasons the writer believes Mr. Aldridge should do this.

_____

_____

_____

_____

_____

3. Identify evidence the writer uses to support his argument.

_____

_____

_____

_____

_____

_____

What's Your Position?

The first step in any kind of argument writing is knowing what you think! Briefly explain whether you agree or disagree with each statement. Give reasons for your position.

1. Requiring students to recycle paper would help improve our environment.

_____

_____

_____

_____

2. Our school wastes too much electricity. Turning off lights when classrooms are empty would solve this problem.

_____

_____

_____

_____

3. Using plastic forks and knives is wasteful. Our school should provide real tableware in the cafeteria.

_____

_____

_____

_____

4. Dropping a few pieces of litter in the school parking lot won't do much harm.

_____

_____

_____

_____

5. To help reduce air pollution, all students should be required to ride their bikes to school.

_____

_____

_____

_____

Plan a Persuasive Business Letter

Use pages 181–182 to plan your persuasive business letter.

1. Think About Your Audience and Purpose
Knowing who your audience is and why you're writing will help you choose effective arguments and evidence for your letter. Fill in the FATP chart for your letter.

FATP Chart

Form: _____

Audience: _____

Topic: _____

Purpose: _____

_____

2. Plan to Appeal to Your Reader's Logic
Plan to back up your point of view with two or three solid reasons. Put them in order from strongest to weakest or from weakest to strongest.

Reason 1

Reason 2

Reason 3

Now plan how you'll support your reasons with evidence, such as facts, statistics, and examples.

Argument	Evidence

3. Plan to Appeal to Your Readers' Emotions

A good letter can use language that appeals to readers' emotions. Think about some effective phrases and sentences you might use. Jot them down here.

Persuasive Language You Might Use

Are there any personal examples that you might use to appeal to readers' emotions? Jot down some ideas here.

Personal Examples You Might Use

Draft a Persuasive Business Letter

Use your plan from pages 181–182 to write the first draft of your persuasive business letter.

Drafting Checklist

☐ Include the date, a greeting and closing, and the writer's and reader's addresses.

☐ Clearly state what you want the reader to do.

☐ Give two to four supporting reasons.

☐ Support reasons with facts and evidence.

☐ Use a formal, respectful tone.

Revise a Persuasive Business Letter

1. Use the checklist to evaluate this draft of a business letter. What changes are needed?

_____

_____

_____

_____

_____

Revising Checklist

☐ Are all the parts of a business letter included?

☐ Are your main arguments stated clearly?

☐ Do you include enough supporting reasons and evidence?

☐ Is the tone formal and respectful?

2. Revise the draft. Use revising marks to show your changes.

Revising

MARK	WHAT IT MEANS
∧	Insert something.
↶	Move to here.
⌐	Replace with this.
ℒ	Take out.
¶	Make a new paragraph.

Dear Mayor Reiss:

I am writing about ways to improve our community center. The center offers weekend classes for students. The center could offer an astronomy class. Many middle school students would sign up.

Some students don't like science. An astronomy class might spark their interest. Thank you for considering this suggestion.

Sincerely,

Kira Pradham

Kira Pradham

3. Now use the checklist to help you revise the draft of your business letter on pages 183–184.

Edit and Proofread

Grammar Workout: Check Prepositional Phrases

Enrich each sentence with a prepositional phrase. Use the preposition suggested in parentheses or another one of your choice.

SOME COMMON PREPOSITIONS			
above	around	below	for
between	on	over	under

1. The children looked up. **(at)**

_____

2. There were thousands of stars. **(in)**

_____

3. They imagined lines connecting them. **(to)**

_____

4. They saw a giant bear in the sky. **(above)**

_____

Spelling Workout: Check Sound-Alike Words

Write the correct form of the sound-alike word in the blank.

1. I went _____ the planetarium yesterday.
     two/to/too

2. I don't know _____ much about exploding stars; I want to learn more.
     two/to/too

3. What was _____ favorite part of the tour?
     you're/your

4. I hope _____ interested in planets now, too.
     you're/your

5. _____ was a gift shop at the planetarium.
there/their/they're

6. _____ T-shirts were cool, but I bought a picture instead.
there/their/they're

7. When some stars die, they can become black _____.
                                        wholes/holes

8. My little brother slept through the _____ show.
                                   whole/hole

Mechanics Workout: Check Parentheses and Dashes

Rewrite each sentence with correct parentheses and dashes.

1. I learned a lot at the planetarium (it was a very interesting place).

_____

2. I learned a lot about galaxies (my favorite subject.)

_____

3. Galaxies contain many celestial bodies, stars, planets, and satellites.

_____

4. Of all the activities at the planetarium there's a lot I enjoyed looking through
the telescope the most.

_____

_____

Check Grammar, Spelling, and Mechanics

**Proofread the passage. Correct errors in spelling and in the use of parentheses
and dashes. Insert prepositional phrases to add more details.**

Editing and Proofreading Marks	
∧	Insert something.
∧	Add a comma.
∧	Add a semicolon.
⊙	Add a period.
⊙	Add a colon.
ᵛᵛ ᵛᵛ	Add quotation marks.
ᵛ	Add an apostrophe.
≡	Capitalize.
╱	Make lower case.
℘	Delete.
¶	Make new paragraph.
◯	Check spelling.
⌅	Replace with this.
∼	Change order.
#	Insert space.
⌣	Close up.

Last weekend my dad took my brother and me to a special
place outside of town. We went far away. We saw the stars!
Their were millions of them.

Dad showed us the Milky Way. (The Milky Way is our
galaxy. I could also sea constellations the Big Dipper and
Ursa Major that I'd never seen before. Dad said that sailors
used to use the stars to steer they're ships at knight.

I loved looking! You usually can't see them.

Edit and Proofread Your Persuasive Business Letter

Now edit and proofread your work.

Remember to Check

☐ prepositional phrases
☐ spelling sound-alike words
☐ parentheses and dashes
☐ _____
☐ _____

1. Use a checklist as you edit and proofread. Add things you are working on to the checklist.

2. Look to see which errors are marked most often. Jot down your top three trouble spots.

_____

_____

_____

3. Ask your teacher about ways to fix these mistakes, or check out the Grammar Handbook for information.

Focus on Spelling

Improve your spelling by following these steps.

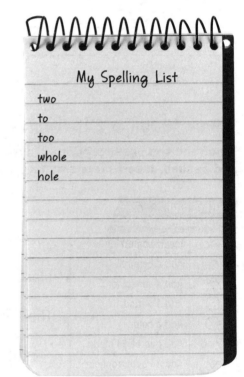

1. Create a personal spelling list. Record words that you misspelled. Look up the correct spelling in the dictionary and add these words to **My Spelling List**.

2. Pick twelve words. Focus on four words each day. Write your words before each meal and check the spelling. At the end of the week, try writing all twelve words.

3. Have a partner stand with his or her back to the board. List your partner's spelling words on the board. Say each word and ask your partner to spell it. Then switch roles.

4. Organize your words into different lists. List them from shortest word to longest word. Next list them from easiest to hardest. Try listing them in reverse alphabetical order.

5. Invent your own acronyms. Think of a word that begins with each letter. The words in the correct order should be easy for you to remember. For example:

Spelling word	**Acronym**
ocean	**o**ctopus, **c**oral, **e**el **a**re **n**ear

Editorial

What makes this editorial a good model?
Read the editorial and answer the questions.

Bring the Steel Drum Band to Hayden Middle School

Did you know that our town has its very own steel drum band? I do, because my father founded it. The band is run out of a local church serving many immigrants from the Caribbean. It has already won music awards across our state. This summer the band will tour the country, but it has never played a concert at one of our schools before. I think a steel drum concert at our school would be a great way to teach our students about Caribbean music.

Having a steel drum concert at our school would show students an instrument that they may not know too much about. It may even inspire them to pick up the steel drums themselves. It will also give students a chance to hear the steel drum band before the rest of the country does. Finally, as our history teacher Ms. Kay points out, Caribbean Heritage Month is this June. A steel drum concert would be a fun and educational way to end our school year.

If you agree that it's important to spread the steel drum music to our schools, let's propose the idea to our school principal at the next student council meeting. Together, we can put together a steel drum celebration.

Feature Checklist

A good editorial

☐ clearly states the writer's opinion in the beginning of the piece

☐ gives convincing evidence to support the opinion

☐ includes a conclusion that restates the opinion, and may tell what others can do to help.

1. What is the writer's argument?

_____

_____

_____

_____

2. What evidence does the writer give to support the argument in the second paragraph?

_____

_____

_____

_____

3. How does the writer wrap up her ideas in the conclusion?

_____

_____

_____

_____

Plan an Editorial

Use page 190 to plan your editorial.

1. Choose a Topic to Write About.
Remember that an editorial expresses an opinion. You should pick a topic you feel strongly about so you can make a clear and detailed argument.

2. Decide on Your Audience and Purpose.
As you write, keep in mind that you are trying to convince your readers. Include facts and details that will make your argument more believable, and stay on topic.

3. Fill in the FATP chart.

FATP Chart

Form: _____

Audience: _____

Topic: _____

Purpose: _____

_____

4. To plan your editorial, write your topic sentence. Then list details and reasons that will support your argument.

Draft an Editorial

Use the plan from page 190 to write the first draft of your editorial.

Drafting Checklist

- [ ] State your argument clearly in the beginning.
- [ ] Support your argument with evidence.
- [ ] Wrap up your ideas in a strong conclusion.

_____

_____

_____

_____

_____

_____

_____

_____

_____

_____

_____

_____

_____

_____

_____

_____

_____

_____

_____

_____

_____

_____

_____

_____

_____

_____

_____

_____

_____

Revise an Editorial

1. Use the checklist to evaluate this draft of an editorial. What changes are needed?

_____

_____

_____

_____

_____

Revising Checklist

☐ Is your argument stated clearly?

☐ Do your sentences flow together well? Can you combine any sentences?

☐ Did you include enough evidence?

2. Revise this draft. Use revising marks to show your changes.

Revising

MARK	WHAT IT MEANS
∧	Insert something.
↺	Move to here.
⌐	Replace with this.
⌐	Take out.
¶	Make a new paragraph.

Let's Celebrate Our Local Music

Last week, our local museum put out a call for new show ideas. I think we should put on a show about music. It would be about local music. It would celebrate this music.

Our town has a lot of local music to celebrate. Our school jazz band just won a state award. Many members of our immigrant communities are also talented musicians. Clyde Lin, who runs Shout Practice Studio, has rented rooms to local musicians from many countries. He has met bagpipe players from Ireland, pan flute players from Peru, and a mariachi band from Mexico.

3. Now use the checklist to help you revise the draft of your editorial on pages 191–192.

Edit and Proofread

Grammar Workout: Check for Complete Sentences

Make complete sentences. Add a subject or a predicate, or join nearby sentences.

1. Is a very good piano player.

_____

2. Our grandmother.

_____

3. She has a beautiful baby grand piano. In her living room.

_____

4. Plays it every day.

_____

5. Grandmother likes to play for us. At parties. At other family gatherings.

_____

Spelling Workout: Check for Tricky Consonant Sounds

Circle the correct spelling of the word in each sentence.

1. I was nervous about Chen's performance. I was sitting on the **ege/edge** of my seat.

2. I **know/now** how hard he worked on his piece.

3. I took a great picture of Chen with my **camera/kamera**.

4. I had to **doge/dodge** the spotlight when I got up to take the picture.

5. I almost got **wrapped/rapped** up in the extension cord on the way back to my seat.

Edit and Proofread, continued

Mechanics Workout: Check Capitalization and Style

Use editing marks from the chart below to fix the capitalization and style errors in each sentence.

1. On memorial day, Chen played at a community Picnic.

2. The crowd loved his rendition of Yankee Doodle Dandy.

3. A local TV show, called *"Around Town,"* broadcasted his performance.

4. An opera singer sang with him as he played a selection from Georges Bizet's opera *"Carmen."*

Check Grammar, Spelling, and Mechanics

Proofread the passage. Check the spelling and the use of complete sentences and capitalization. Correct the mistakes.

Editing and Proofreading Marks	
∧	Insert something.
⋏	Add a comma.
⋏	Add a semicolon.
⊙	Add a period.
⊙	Add a colon.
∨ ∨	Add quotation marks.
∨	Add an apostrophe.
≡	Capitalize.
/	Make lower case.
℘	Delete.
¶	Make new paragraph.
◯	Check spelling.
⌒	Replace with this.
∽	Change order.
#	Insert space.
‿	Close up.

Andi and I enjoyed the valentine's day koncert. Played really well. The piece beautiful to me. I can't believe how much he practiced. He plays the symphony *"Rhapsody in Blue"* gust perfectly now.

He will the famous Chen Wu one day! When he plays on *the tonight show,* I hope he'll still speack to us. I asked him if he would. "Of kourse I will," he replied.

Wish I could play an instrument like that. Chen must be a musical jenius!

Edit and Proofread Your Editorial

Now edit and proofread your work.

Remember to Check

☐ complete sentences

☐ spelling of tricky consonant sounds

☐ capitalization and style

☐ _____

☐ _____

1. Use a checklist as you edit and proofread. Add things you are working on to the checklist.

2. Look to see which errors are marked most often. Jot down your top three trouble spots.

_____

_____

_____

3. Ask your teacher about ways to fix these mistakes, or check out the Grammar Handbook for information.

Focus on Spelling

Improve your spelling by following these steps.

1. Create a personal spelling list. Record words that you misspelled. Look up the correct spelling in the dictionary and add these words to **My Spelling List**.

2. Pick twelve words. Write each word four times. First, write it in all lowercase letters. Next, write it in all capital letters. After that, write the vowels in lowercase and the consonants in uppercase. Last, write the word using fancy letters that you create on your own.

3. Work with a partner to play **I'm Thinking of a Spelling Word**. Take turns giving each other clues. Some clues might be *I'm thinking of a word that rhymes with . . .*, *I'm thinking of a word that begins with . . .*, or *I'm thinking of a word that means . . .* With each clue, the answer should include the word and its spelling.

4. With a partner, play a scrambled-letter game. Take each other's spelling words and write them in scrambled form. See who can unscramble all the words first.

5. Use an audio recorder and record your words and their spelling. Then listen to your recording, checking to see that you spelled each word correctly.

My Spelling List

camera
pick
genius
fudge
know

Literary Response

What makes this literary response a good model?
Read the response and answer the questions.

Feature Checklist

A good literary response tells

☐ the name of the work and the author

☐ what the work is mostly about

☐ how you feel about the work and why

☐ reasons why you liked or did not like the work

☐ details from the work that support your opinion

☐ something important you learned from the work.

Lois Lowry's *The Giver*
by Donnell Hughes

The Giver, by Lois Lowry, tells the story of Jonas, a boy living in a world that seems to be perfect. Everyone in his community is treated equally. The problems we have in our world seem to have disappeared. When Jonas gets his adult job, everything changes. Jonas learns what is wrong with his world. He must figure out what he can do to change it.

I really like this novel because it made me think. Sometimes, we all wish we lived in a world without any problems. This book gave me a chance to see what it would be like if we could get rid of anything that seems wrong. The problems would not really be gone. They would just be hidden. The people in Jonas's town have to do horrible things to keep the town looking perfect. Everyone must fit in, and those who don't fit in have to suffer. I would rather live in a world with differences. Sometimes I disagree with others, but at least I am not forced to act like everyone else.

It's not just people who must all be the same in *The Giver*. The weather stays the same all the time. Sure, it would be great if I never had to worry about rain or sleet. But the people in the town never get to go sledding, hear a storm, or see a rainbow. It sounds pretty boring.

1. What information does the writer give in the first paragraph?

_____

_____

_____

_____

2. What does the writer say *The Giver* is mostly about?

_____

_____

_____

_____

_____

3. How does the writer feel about Jonas's world? How do you know?

_____

_____

_____

_____

_____

_____

_____

_____

Reading this book let me see my world in a new way. Jonas's job is to receive memories of things that are gone. That means he sees things like snow and holidays for the first time. I didn't realize how exciting those things could be until I saw them through Jonas's eyes. Jonas also sees war for the first time. I got to see how horrible war would seem if it were a new idea. That made it easier to understand the reason for the town.

Even though Jonas comes from a different world, I enjoyed reading about him. I could relate to some of the things he was feeling. Sometimes, we all feel like we have to fit in even if we don't want to. Also, Jonas is twelve years old and goes through a lot of the same things I have gone through growing up. Liking Jonas made me care about what happened to him and to his town.

Lois Lowry has done a great job. She created a novel that made me appreciate my own world, even with all its problems. I recommend it.

4. What reasons does the writer give for why he liked the book?

_____

_____

_____

_____

5. What has the writer learned from the book?

_____

_____

_____

_____

6. What does the writer do in the last paragraph?

_____

_____

_____

_____

Find Out What You Think

1. What have you read about artistic expression? Which works sparked a reaction or strong opinion?

_____

_____

_____

_____

_____

2. Track your responses for each work. Use the chart to help you decide what you think about it.

Literature
Opinions and Reactions

What's good about it?	What could be better?

Would I recommend this to other people? Why or why not?

Support Your Statements with Specifics

1. Back up your opinions about a book. Look back through the book, story, or literary work. Gather evidence for your opinions.

Title of Work: _____

Author: _____

Opinion 1:

Text Evidence:

Opinion 2:

Text Evidence:

Opinion 3:

Text Evidence:

Support Your Statements with Specifics, continued

2. Dig deeper. Find text evidence and exact quotations or dialogue in the work to support two opinions on page 200.

Opinion:

Text Evidence:

Specfic Text Detail:	Exact Quotation:

Opinion:

Text Evidence:

Specfic Text Detail:	Exact Quotation:

Give Your Opinion

Tell what kind of appeal the writer uses in each example. Explain why the example is effective.

I liked how *The Giver* described a different kind of world. If I were Jonas, I'd like that everyone is treated equally and there are no problems. But who wants to live in a place when everything is the same day after day? Don't most of us want some variety? *The Giver* helps me appreciate my own world.

_____

_____

_____

_____

_____

The Giver is a wonderful book. It won't be long until you think of Jonas as your best friend. You'll be eager to know what Jonas learns. By the last chapter, you'll be biting your nails as you wait to see what happens.

_____

_____

_____

_____

_____

Put It All Together

Read the literary response carefully and answer the questions.

Kate Thompson's
The New Policeman
by Shana White

The New Policeman is a novel by Kate Thompson. It takes readers on a journey through Irish music and legend. Teens who like music will like *The New Policeman*. So will teens who just like a good story. I thought it was an interesting and surprising read.

This book is about JJ Liddy. JJ is a teenage boy from Ireland. He comes from a family of musicians, and he plays the fiddle. His family hosts concerts for everyone from the village. JJ's life is good. But there's a problem: Time is passing too quickly. There's never enough time to get everything done. For her birthday, JJ's mom asks for more time. So JJ decides to find out where the time has gone.

Things really get exciting when JJ starts his search for time. He discovers that time has been leaking out of his world. JJ finds his way into a strange, magical land. This is the world where the time has gone. The people JJ meets there seem to be ordinary musicians. But are they more than that? JJ must uncover their secret. Then, he has to bring time back to his own world. JJ's job seems impossible! Time is literally running out. Luckily, JJ has friends, family, and music to help him.

Feature Checklist

- [ ] the name of the work and the author
- [ ] what the work is mostly about
- [ ] how you feel about the work and why
- [ ] reasons why you liked or did not like the work
- [ ] details from the work that support your opinion
- [ ] something important you learned from the work.

1. Underline the sentence that states the writer's overall opinion of the book.

2. Circle key details about the book's characters and plot that the writer uses as evidence to support her opinion.

3. Did the writer summarize the plot well? Explain what the problem is in the story, and explain what the main character must do.

_____

_____

_____

_____

_____

_____

_____

Music is an important part of the story. Each chapter ends with an Irish song. Music is also one link between the real world and the magical world. Readers who are musicians will find it easy to relate to JJ. But all readers will enjoy the musical rhythm of the story. It's easy to imagine the sounds of the songs that the characters play. When you read this book, it's almost like you're listening to a CD at the same time!

I really enjoyed reading *The New Policeman*. On his journey, JJ learns that things aren't always as they appear. Things that seem impossible can happen with no explanation. JJ's love of music and his love for his family help him make sense of these surprising events. I think this is a lesson that everyone can appreciate. Most people don't go on amazing adventures. However, we all need help to get through tough times. I'm not an Irish fiddle player, but music is as important to me as it is to JJ. Playing the guitar helps me feel better when I'm upset. Like the characters in the story, I can also ask my family for help.

The New Policeman is a great adventure story. It also has an important message: It reminds us that the things and people we love can help us succeed.

4. **What other thoughts and opinions does the writer express about the book?**

_____

_____

_____

_____

_____

5. **What life lesson did the writer learn from the book?**

_____

_____

_____

_____

_____

_____

6. **Now that you have read this literary response, do you want to read the book? Why or why not?**

_____

_____

_____

_____

_____

_____

_____

Plan a Literary Response

Use pages 205–206 to plan your literary response.

1. What book would you like to write about? On the lines below, make a list of possible books. Consider each book. Then choose a book to write about. Circle the title of the book you choose.

_____

_____

_____

_____

_____

_____

_____

_____

2. What are your opinions and thoughts about the book? Use the space below to organize your ideas.

Book _____

Opinions and Reactions

_____

_____

_____

_____

_____

_____

_____

_____

_____

_____

_____

3. Now plan the layers of your literary response. Use the "cake" diagram below to take notes about what you plan to cover in each layer.

Title:

Author:

Opinion:

Summary and supporting details:

Life lesson or personal response:

Draft a Literary Response

Use your plan from pages 205–206 to write the first draft of
your literary response.

**Drafting
Checklist**

- ☐ Identify the
  title and author
  of the work at
  the beginning of
  your response.

- ☐ Explain what the
  work is mostly
  about.

- ☐ Describe how
  you feel about
  the work and
  why.

- ☐ Give reasons
  why you liked
  or disliked the
  work.

- ☐ Provide details
  from the work
  that support
  your opinion.

- ☐ Tell something
  important you
  learned from the
  work.

Draft a Literary Response, continued

Revise a Literary Response

1. Use the checklist to evaluate this draft of a literary response. What changes are needed?

_____

_____

_____

_____

_____

Revising Checklist

- [ ] Does the writing tell what the work is mostly about?
- [ ] Is the writer's opinion clear?
- [ ] Are there enough examples or specific details to support the writer's opinion?
- [ ] Is it clear what the writer learned from the work?
- [ ] Can any text be consolidated so it gets right to the point?

2. Revise the draft. Use revising marks to show your changes.

Revising

MARK	WHAT IT MEANS
∧	Insert something.
↶	Move to here.
∧‾	Replace with this.
___ℓ	Take out.
¶	Make a new paragraph.

Nightsong: The Legend of Orpheus and Eurydice

Nightsong by Michael Cadnum retells the ancient love story of Orpheus and Eurydice. Orpheus is a musician and a poet. He loves Eurydice. Unfortunately, she is bitten by a snake. The snake bite kills her.

Orpheus can't accept her death. He travels to the Underworld to find her. There, he uses his songs to convince the god Pluto to let Eurydice live. Pluto agrees. But here's the tough part. If Orpheus looks at her, Eurydice must stay in the Underworld. On their return, Orpheus can't resist. He loses her forever.

Although it was sad, I enjoyed this story. I felt for Orpheus. Even though it's a sad story, it shows the power of love.

3. Now use the checklist to help you revise the draft of your literary response on pages 207–208.

Edit and Proofread

Grammar Workout: Check Compound Sentences

Combine each pair of sentences to make a compound sentence.
Be sure to use *and, but,* or *or* correctly.

1. Billie was scared to be alone in the woods. The animals kept her calm.

_____

2. An owl sat in a tree above her all night. It would hoot every few minutes.

_____

3. Billie thought it might be trying to talk to her. Maybe it was talking to other animals.

_____

4. Billie listened closely. She couldn't understand the owl's message.

_____

Spelling Workout: Check Suffixes

Add the suffix *–ful* to these words.

1. fancy _____   **3.** wonder _____   **5.** mind _____

2. pity _____   **4.** peace _____   **6.** use _____

Add the suffix *–able* to these words.

7. like _____   **9.** fashion _____   **11.** read _____

8. enjoy _____   **10.** depend _____   **12.** desire _____

Add the suffix *–y* to these words.

13. rain _____   **15.** mud _____   **17.** smog _____

14. sun _____   **16.** stick _____   **18.** haze _____

Edit and Proofread, continued

Mechanics Workout: Check Titles and Quotes

Edit each sentence. Use the editing marks from the chart below to add or remove quotation marks and fix errors in capitalization.

1. I really enjoyed Jean Craighead George's book, *the talking earth*.

2. George also wrote a book called *everglades*.

3. George's first line in the book is, "I'm going to tell you a story. A story about a river.

4. In the story, the narrator says, The grass clatters like a trillion swords.

5. This book reminded me of the Sioux poem The Earth Only.

Check Grammar, Spelling, and Mechanics

Proofread the passage. Check the spelling, compound sentences, titles, and quotations. Correct the mistakes.

Editing and Proofreading Marks	
∧	Insert something.
⋏	Add a comma.
⋏	Add a semicolon.
⊙	Add a period.
⊙	Add a colon.
⌄⌄	Add quotation marks.
⌄	Add an apostrophe.
≡	Capitalize.
/	Make lower case.
⌫	Delete.
¶	Make new paragraph.
◯	Check spelling.
⌐	Replace with this.
∼	Change order.
#	Insert space.
⌢	Close up.

I think Jean Craighead George's writing is beautyful. I really want to read her book titled *"Julie"*. It is the first book in a noteable series. The other books are *Julie of the wolves* and *Julie's wolf pack*. The book tells about the friendily relationship Julie has with wolves. Julie becomes connected with one particular wolf, but calls him Kapu. Kapu is a very thoughtfull wolf. But Kapu "must go away. If Julie's father sees the wolf, or he will kill it. I think this book will be enjoiable. I will check it out of the library, but I will buy it at the bookstore.

Edit and Proofread Your Literary Response

Now edit and proofread your work.

Remember to Check

☐ compound sentences

☐ spelling of words with suffixes

☐ titles and quotations

☐ _____

☐ _____

1. Use a checklist as you edit and proofread.
Add things you are working on to the checklist.

2. Look to see which errors are marked most often.
Jot down your top three trouble spots.

_____

_____

_____

3. Ask your teacher about ways to fix these mistakes, or check out the
Grammar Handbook for information.

Focus on Spelling

Improve your spelling by following these steps.

1. Create a personal spelling list. Record words that you
misspelled. Look up the correct spelling in the dictionary
and add these words to **My Spelling List**.

2. Pick twelve words. Make each word look interesting and
special by tracing it five times. Write the word in one
color. Then trace it four more times in four different
colors. Say each letter to yourself as you trace it.

3. Work with a partner to play **Spelling Catch**. Pitch words
to each other by saying "Here's the windup. Here's the
pitch. The word is . . ." Take turns pitching. The first
"batter" to spell ten words correctly wins.

4. Write each spelling word three times. The first time, just
write the word. The second time, write it and then circle all the consonants.
The third time, write it and circle all the vowels.

5. Play **Memory** to help you remember your words. Write each spelling word on
two different index cards. Mix up the cards and place them face down. Turn
the cards over two at a time. Your goal is to find the matching cards. Say and
spell the words on the cards you turn over. If you make a match, remove those
cards from the game. You've won when you've removed all the cards.

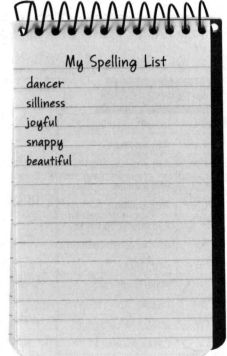

My Spelling List

dancer
silliness
joyful
snappy
beautiful

Publish, Share, and Reflect

Publish and Share Your Literary Response

**Check the final formats you used to publish your literary response.
Then answer the following questions.**

Publishing

What was the final format of your project?	How did you share your project?
☐ Wrote it neatly by hand	☐ Shared it with a large group
☐ Typed it on a computer	☐ Shared it with a small group

---

1. Whether you published it by hand or on the computer, what did you do to dress up your final project?

_____

_____

_____

_____

2. How did you share your work? What did you learn through sharing your work?

_____

_____

_____

_____

_____

_____

_____

_____

_____

_____

_____

_____

Reflect on Your Literary Response

Read your literary response. Then answer questions 1–6.

1. What do you like best about your work? _____

_____

_____

2. What did you do well? _____

_____

_____

3. What could you improve about your work? _____

_____

_____

_____

4. What did you discover about yourself as you wrote about a literary work? _____

_____

_____

5. What can you do to make your writing more interesting to others? _____

_____

_____

6. Will you add your literary response to your Writing Portfolio? Explain
your decision.

❑ Yes, I will add this to my Writing Portfolio.

_____

_____

❑ No, I will not add this to my Writing Portfolio.

_____

_____